F

ENDORSEMENTS

"I find Laurel Hobbs' book fascinating. It's a really good read. If you are looking for hope, inspiration and insight, I encourage you to grab a copy of *Broken and Made Whole*. Enjoy the little epiphanies you will have as you follow the stories of this beautiful woman doing some beautiful work in the world."

Jack Canfield
Renowned speaker, coach, and best-selling author and co-creator of the Chicken Soup for the Soul *series*

"Rarely will you have the privilege of becoming invited into the soul of an author as their autobiography is shared... the soul I refer to is the mind, will and emotions of the writer. You may at times read a remarkable story but seldom do the words impact your own life to any significant depth.

Not so with Laurel Hobbs' *Broken and Made Whole*! She has been willing to pull back the curtains which safely covered the windows of her life and bare her soul for all to see: that BEAUTY can come out of ashes, JOY really can come out of mourning and PRAISE really can overcome despair.

In reading her story it will be as though you are actually experiencing her thoughts, her emotions and her choices… you are really there and will laugh and cry along with her. Not only that, you will appreciate the ability to hear God's voice and the choice to obey which brings untold blessing, healing and fruitfulness."

Mary Audrey Raycroft
Teaching Pastor, Catch The Fire Toronto, author of Releasers of Life, *keynote speaker*

Wow! What a journey Laurel has had in moving from brokenness to wholeness. I read this book in one sitting. As one who has known Laurel, Bob and their four sons, as one who has lived the journey of Jack's life with them, I found this book very emotional. While not trying to give it away, the chapter on the graduation of their son, Jack, brought me to tears. It was an easy, fun read, yet so emotional, I began my own introspection asking the same questions of myself as Laurel's. I would highly recommend this book for everyone but especially those who have had trauma and tragedy as part of their past.

Steve Long
Senior Leader of Catch The Fire Church (Toronto), Author of My Healing Belongs to Me, The Faith Zone, *etc.*

Having known Laurel for over 20 years, and having walked through many of the adventures in this book, I can attest to the fact that her story is real!

I pray that as you read this, you will learn to avoid many pitfalls on your journey to become closer to the Lord, thereby providing redemption for all of the trials and tribulations that Laurel and her son, Jack, went through.

Elaine Rose

This is a must-read of a mother, wife and dear pastor and her amazing journey with her beautiful son, Jack. The journey vividly demonstrates the support of the comforting love of Daddy God. I remember personally hearing the stories of Jack that glorified our God and brought him great honour from the time he was a little boy right up to the time heaven saw him dancing before the throne of the King of Kings. What joy both Laurel and Bob had with Jack. It is unbelievable to think that not one single night of his life did Jack ever go to bed worried about being alone without parental oversight. I feel so blessed to know and to continue to know Laurel and to recommend this masterpiece.

Please take the time to read this truly inspiring autobiography. Laurel's desire and her prayer are that you would, in the same way, come to know God as she learned to love and know God as she cared for Jack. Friends, as you read, please hear the message that the Saviour has died for you so that you would have eternal life. For both Laurel and her family, Jack was born and lived so that they would encounter Jesus Christ as the way, the truth and the life. May you read and encounter Him for yourself.

Bruno Ierullo
Author of The Double Portion Life
Global Ambassador & Founding Pastor CTFN

This book is so refreshing as Laurel clearly explains the anointed processes God used to get her free of significant life trauma and move her past the effects. Her story will make you cry and rejoice and give honour to God.

She faced many tragic and unusual events but also many common to us all. The details of God's guidance, while allowing her to touch others in the midst, is illuminating. We laughed and cried throughout her story. We especially love the congregation of the ducks and how God spoke to her through them. This is one of the major strengths of the book – revealing patterns of how to process "life" and move toward a more healthy, ready example of Jesus' life shining through us.

Catherine and Don James
Pastors of New Life Church,
Founders of His Love Ministries,
Board Members, Global Outpouring

BROKEN
and Made
WHOLE

*A Mother's Unexpected Discovery
of the Supernatural*

LAUREL HOBBS

WESTBOW
PRESS®
A DIVISION OF THOMAS NELSON
& ZONDERVAN

WestBow Press books may be ordered through booksellers or by contacting:

WestBow Press
A Division of Thomas Nelson & Zondervan
1663 Liberty Drive
Bloomington, IN 47403
www.westbowpress.com
844-714-3454

Scripture taken from the New King James Version® Copyright © 1982 by Thomas Nelson. Used by permission. All rights reserved.

ISBN: 978-1-6642-4872-4 (sc)
ISBN: 978-1-6642-4873-1 (hc)
ISBN: 978-1-6642-4871-7 (e)

Library of Congress Control Number: 2021922225

Print information available on the last page.

WestBow Press rev. date: 11/08/2021

CONTENTS

Proverbs 3:5-6

Trust in the Lord with all your heart,
And lean not on your own understanding:
In all your ways acknowledge Him,
And He shall direct your paths.

INTRODUCTION

To be honest, I was unaware that my life lacked a visionary dream. I was floating along in something that I assumed was a fairly normal, North American life. I was pleased to have and took pride in our family. I worked hard within our home every day, but I cannot say that I was inspired. This is the story of my being broken and then made whole.

The brokenness came with my pregnancy and the birth of our fourth son, Jack, who was born with cerebral palsy, as well as many other disabilities. This resulted in our child being unable to do much of anything. Caring for Jack and the challenges of life became monumental.

My life and emotions seemed to sink into a depressing resignation and fear of the future. In an outward sense, I knew that I projected and that others perceived me as a cheerful, friendly, and outgoing person. However, the bankruptcy of my inner thought life became increasingly clear to me in the midst of my personal crisis. Then while facing the worst and in the light of the gospel of Jesus Christ's truth, I was miraculously restored to a fruitful and joyful realignment of activity and desire in my life.

Today, I do everything with all my might because I can, and you can too! I am grateful for the basic abilities that were given to me. I have learned to be inspired in life, and I am loved by the Holy Spirit. His strength and excellence guide me through each day and lead me in a way that providentially sets up, connects, and adds to my next adventure and victory. My life is fulfilling.

I paraphrase Proverb 23:7, which teaches us, "As a man thinks in his heart, so is he." I want a life that is worth living, and I am sure you do too. Our lives can only manifest the condition and integrity of our own hearts. In His love, the Great Physician and our Father offers to take our wounded hearts, soften them, and transform them so that once again, we are able to be sensitive to God and each other.

As a mother of a disabled son, my goal and desire in writing this autobiographical journey are that it would bring revelation and save you, dear reader, years and tears. Because heavenly Father's holy and imperishable seed dwells within us, His divine nature and eternal, immeasurable power become available to us. The anointing that we need to be made whole and overcome the difficulties and great challenges of life is found in the presence and power of our almighty God and faith in Christ Jesus.

Thus the will and purpose of God for each one of us becomes more manifested until we become a voice that is amplified in the earth. Are you aware that you are valuable and loved and have a wonderful destiny awaiting you? Please don't miss it! As you learn about and experience the revelation of my journey, I pray that your own restoration will be accelerated.

Today, my husband and I have been blessed with seven beautiful grandchildren, who are the fruit of our oldest three sons. I am an ordained pastor. I have been leading a home church and overseeing weekly and monthly Christian women's meetings for many years. Over the past twenty-five years, I have been trained by many anointed people and ministries. I am now involved at a leadership level with End-Time Handmaidens and Servants, which has been recently renamed Global Outpouring, as well as United In Christ. I am also a chairperson on the board of directors of Signet Christian School in Toronto, Canada.

My hope and prayer is that this written account of some of God's strange but wonderful dealings with me, Jack, and several others will

- Encourage you to believe in your heavenly Father and that He desires your fellowship
- Help you to yield to your own Spirit-led journey through faith in Christ Jesus
- Lead you to embrace His love for you on a personal and intimate level

As you surrender to His love, all heaven will be working on your behalf to bring you out of your brokenness and into your purpose and destiny. His heart of love is the source of all true wholeness. He did this for me and wants to do the same for you. Enjoy the journey!

CHAPTER 1

Going Beyond Crisis and Stepping into the Light

Do you like epic stories as much as I do? Whether those stories are real-life or fictional accounts, most of us enjoy the borrowed thrill of a heroic journey, where someone comes out of a pit of seemingly insurmountable circumstances to a triumphal, joyful, and purposeful resolution. I honestly never suspected my life might follow that pattern, but it did.

Recently, I felt the Holy Spirit nudge me to write about my journey. I went from being a worldly pseudo-intellectually secular feminist to a radical (or so some consider me), committed, born-again, and Christian pastor. The recent COVID-19 lockdown provided the necessary time and space to write.

My motive and ongoing desire are that my story will provide signposts and truths that will save some of you from wasting as many years as I did because I didn't know about the readily available blessing and favor of God. Our heavenly Father really does love to bless and empower each member of His family. If you are a breathing human being, His invitation is extended to you. I believe that as you consider the following experiences and truths, at some deep level, you will absorb and birth your own supernatural revelations. Thus you will do great exploits and lay claim to your own fulfilling victories.

My transformational journey from brokenness to wholeness began with the planned cesarean birth of our fourth son, Jack, on August 10, 1993. After this planned and surgical delivery, the pediatrician informed me of Jack's high Apgar score. It was the best newborn Apgar score of all four boys, but I was not convinced that this was the truth. I had been forewarned in an unusual and dark dream during the pregnancy that he would have extensive abnormalities. Had I known how to pray, I believe that I could have overcome and undone much, if not all, of the bad reports and outcomes that I had seen in my mind. Unfortunately, I was ignorant. The fear that was produced by my dream and its prediction gripped me. In Hosea 4:6, God laments, "My people are destroyed for lack of knowledge." Indeed, that was me.

A season of appointments with specialists and tests to determine the extent of all the realities of Jack's condition followed. At that time, I could only see a lifetime of difficulty, dysfunction, and sadness for both Jack and me. The diagnosis was primarily cerebral palsy, but there was much more. Jack had a broken body, and I had a broken heart. As if in a prison, I could see and hear a barred metal door closing to shut me in a prison of my own self-accusations, fears, and despair. I wondered, *What did I do to deserve this?* Sadly, a list came to mind, and I sank lower.

Four months after Jack was born, a close friend phoned and invited me to a Christmas luncheon with her new Bible study group of women. I remained uninterested until she told me that years earlier, the hostess had adopted a baby girl who was later diagnosed with cerebral palsy. A small group of believers had gathered to pray for this baby, and after three months, she had been healed. Now my friend had my attention! It especially helped that the hostess's husband was a judge. I had already taken Jack to a number of "specialists" who seemed more quirky than qualified. I decided that I would go to the Christmas luncheon with my friend and take our son.

The nondenominational Christian women's gathering took place in a nearby home. The women all seemed much older than my friend and me. They sang, read the Christmas story from the Bible, and shared their prayer needs. At the end of their luncheon and meeting, I gathered up my courage. They listened as I launched into my teary questions. "Should I pray for Jack or for me? In fact, I actually don't think I know how to pray." You can imagine my sobs. They gathered around, laid hands on me, and took turns praying. Oh, happy day! For three full days, I experienced an inner miraculous presence of what I can only remember as a strengthening joy.

About a week after the event, the hostess phoned and invited me to pray what she called "The Sinner's Prayer." I repeated a prayer where I repented of my sins, asked for forgiveness, turned, and looked to Jesus Christ as my Lord and Savior. Then she advised me to begin to pray for good parking spaces as a way of building my faith that praying actually worked.

Parking spaces? I thought. At the time, I even wondered whether it was entirely legitimate to be saying prayers over a phone. Today, I can assure you that just about any mode or whimper of a prayer from a true heart is heard in heaven. I was more than ready to repent and follow this new group and the Christian way.

My journey as a disciple began bit by bit. I joined the women in their weekly Bible study. I began to learn what the kingdom of heaven was all about and the possibilities and promises that were available to me as a child of God. I was a seeker and a committed one. My intellectual mind often told me that my pursuit was ridiculous. The Bible and the women challenged me mentally at almost every meeting.

I often had to tell my mind to be quiet and in a childish kind of way, to put my mental reasoning on a shelf to avoid its interference. It was true that my three-day experience of the joy of the Lord had not lasted, but my heart remained hopeful. It was all I had to hold onto. I was willing to yield and be a good student and disciple.

I had just started attending the Bible study when my girlfriend announced that she was being water baptized and thought I might want to join her in this full-immersion experience. I had no understanding of what it meant. So I said, "I do not think this is like a dinner out, but I will go with you as your friend and support you." I also wanted to go because my first Christian mentor, Miriam, who had led me to the Lord on the phone, had arranged it at her church. She is an elegant, retired nurse, who is also very evangelistic, compassionate, and knowledgeable. I always felt totally safe under her tutelage.

When the appointed date arrived, Miriam and her husband waited with me in the pews. We were early because of the baptism preparations being made for the participants. An additional agenda item that night was the honoring of the church's retiring music director, for his faithful worship leadership. What looked like a full symphonic orchestra was rehearsing for this occasion. Its sound was beautiful.

Every time the music played, I would cry uncontrollably, and I could not stop. The tears would only stop when the music stopped. I wondered if I was having a nervous breakdown. I could not talk. Miriam and her husband sat calmly on the long blond-oak pew as if my weeping was the most normal thing in the world. They passed me tissues in a timely, unobtrusive manner.

I watched the baptism and listened to the sermon, but strangely, every time the orchestra's music filled the sanctuary, tears flowed down my face in unbidden streams. When it was all over, I still could not talk. Looking for reassurance, I turned to Miriam. I finally got out the words, "I have to do that!" That was all I could say.

She gave me a beneficent, knowing smile. It was definitely a Holy Spirit moment. Miriam nodded and said, "Fine. I will set it up with the church as soon as I can."

On April 17, 1994, I was to be water baptized. By this time, I had a basic understanding of what it was about. I was acknowledging my sins, my need for forgiveness, and my new faith, which believed that Jesus Christ took all my punishment for me so that I could live and start again as a child of God. My previous life would be left in the baptismal waters of my repentance, and my heavenly Father and the Holy Spirit were honoring and welcoming my desire to be a Christian child of God. I had invited my family because I did not know how to explain the desire that I had to publicly proclaim my faith and my change of heart.

I was taken aback and felt my ignorance when the

church secretary phoned to ask me what worship song I would like them to play while I was being baptized. I confess that at this stage my repertoire of known Christian songs was limited. I chose "Amazing Grace" because it was the only Christian song that I could think of. It was surprisingly appropriate. I had known the tune, but I had not known all the words until that night.

Being sympathetic of what they knew was a stressful situation, no one in my family asked me the reason that I was doing it, although I could see that they were baffled. My husband, children, mother, and two of my sisters attended the ceremony and said very little. Perhaps because my family was there, I was distracted by their reactions. My baptism was not as profound as the first baptism that I had witnessed and cried through. Yet I knew that I had obeyed and that something significant had happened. The strange tearful prompting of the Holy Spirit had opened a fresh way of *being*. I was quietly joyful on the inside—a welcome change.

One night, I was sitting in my room and trying to pray. I was still very influenced by new age thinking and visualizing in the dark. Our imagination is a powerful tool for good or evil, depending on our disposition, desire, and input.

In my inner drama, I could see myself sitting in a little teepee-like temple. Small movie screens were everywhere. It was dark but comfortable. I sat in the dark on the smooth wooden center bench, which reminded me of the ones in large art galleries that I had visited. Relaxed, I could sit and watch the screens and reflect. They were all scenes from different parts of my life. Colors and movements on the multiple screens flashed like jewels. I felt that it was enabling me to see patterns in my life.

Suddenly, the Holy Spirit took over my vision. The top of the teepee opened up like a small version of the SkyDome stadium's roof. A white dove fluttered down. For some reason, I did not pull away or flinch. When it settled on my shoulder and brushed its head and beak against my cheek, I burst into tears! I don't even know what happened within me or how to explain it, but I knew God was there. I knew that He had accepted me and that He was present to help me in my brokenness. It was a precious and comforting revelation.

I was invited by Miriam to join their home-meeting group. I enjoyed my first Bible study. In the beginning, I remember feeling that they were speaking a different language and that I couldn't understand it. It took some time and inner adjustments before I began to comprehend the things that they were talking about. I loved the scriptural stories of faith and miracles; however, when they talked about scriptures that referred to demons, it made me wonder, *Do they really believe in this stuff?* My understanding of the spiritual world was limited, and I still had the doubt of a worldly mind.

The group later took me along to a hotel-room meeting to hear Billy Burke, an American healing evangelist. My husband and baby Jack came as well. After preaching, Billy Burke invited people with chronic pain to come forward for prayer. Against my will, my husband wanted to rush up with Jack in the stroller. I tried to reason with him that it was not our turn. Jack was not in pain. He ignored me and rushed to the front, telling Billy Burke all about Jack's condition.

The man of God reassured him that the baby would be fine. He then turned away from the stroller and put his hands on Bob, who was instantly slain in the Spirit. A man had been strategically placed behind Bob. He caught Bob and guided him to the floor as he fell backward. Bob lay there peacefully on his back, on the platform, and under the power of God. I started to cry. I had been so concerned about correctly following orders that I was still in my chair. I assumed that I had missed God's best for me.

After the meeting ended, Billy Burke invited everyone to stand in a circle. He was going to lay hands on each of us. This really excited me. I would not miss anything after all. After waiting my turn, I too was slain in the Spirit (to my great joy and relief).

Afterward while on our way home, I asked my husband if he still felt anything. He said that he did not. He had been surprised to find himself on the floor in the meeting and not knowing how he got there. I told him that I felt like I had a comforting layer of warm pulsating air around my heart. Today, I realize that it was the presence of the Holy Spirit. I had been filled, even without asking for or understanding it. My weeks of studying and seeking had prepared me for that glorious moment of infilling. My faith was sparking and shooting upward. I was hungry for more.

I began to earnestly read Christian books and my Bible. I was now desperately searching for more of the powerful presence that I had experienced, the revelation of its source, and the manifestation and results of prayer. I was especially eager to understand and utilize scriptural healing prayer. As much and as often as I was able, I prayed for Jack.

My first prayer request was for his eyes because he

could not open his eyelids. The doctors told me that he had a third cranial nerve palsy, which controlled the rotation of his eyes, the dilation of their pupils, and the lifting of the eyelids. These were all problems for Jack. Even worse, his irises were pulled to the outside corners of his eyes. They did not move or dilate. His eyes looked like fish eyes. I think it was the kindness of the Lord that Jack's eyes were swollen shut for the first few days after his birth. The horror of his condition had not been fully evident, but because of my dream, I expected the worst. Now I was contending for transformation and healing.

I started praying intensely. I also taped Jack's eyes open one at a time, in my hope that with some visual stimulation, he would not be blind. I love nature's beauty, and I had studied art, so the idea of him not being able to see was devastating. I told his new ophthalmology surgeon what I was doing, even though I knew that I was abandoning the conventional wisdom of covering one of Jack's eyes at a time. I expected a scornful reply, which would sound something like, "What's the point of that? How stupid." However, he thought for a moment about what I was doing and liked the idea. He gave me surgical tape so that it would not irritate the skin around Jack's eyes so much.

Over the next few months, Jack first opened one eye and then the other, which certainly baffled the doctors. His other problems did not change. As he got older, Jack was able to turn his head and look with the eye that he could open most easily. Much later, a surgery did straighten his eyes out somewhat, but his immediate eyelid improvement was an answer to my prayer request and enough to encourage my faith in God's will to heal. I was determined to continue praying.

When we took Jack to The Hospital for Sick Children (SickKids) to get an opinion from an eye doctor who had said that he would try to straighten Jack's eyes out surgically, his attitude upset me. He said, "If his eyes look more normal, you'll feel better about him." It felt like he drove a knife into my heart. I have forgiven him. I know that he did not mean to offend me, but the cosmetic appearance of Jack was not my concern. Like any mother, I wanted Jack to have a meaningful life.

The doctor said he could do the surgery in the following two weeks. Again I started to cry, and I could not talk about it. My husband set up the appointment, and we left.

When we got home, I was still crying. Bob said, "Pull yourself together. I'll go get the kids." Jack's three older brothers came home from the local school each day for lunch.

I sat in the soft bedroom armchair where I had become accustomed to praying. I said, *Lord, what should I do?* I could not stop crying. In my muddled emotional state, I tried to reason with myself. *I could phone my friend, but what good would that do? I could phone Miriam, my spiritual mother and mentor, but she would say, "Go to the Word!"* So after sucking in a much-needed breath and trying to find faith, I opened my Bible. The pages rested on 1 Samuel 3. I read the wonderful story of the little boy Samuel. He slept in the holy tabernacle of the Lord near the Ark of the Covenant. He was under the tutelage of the high priest Eli.

One night, Samuel heard his name being called. He ran obediently to the high priest, assuming he was being paged for some task. This happened a few times. Finally,

Eli realized that it was the Lord speaking to this young boy, and he instructed Samuel to reply, "Speak, Lord, for Your servant hears."

I knew the rest of the story but now paused in an attempt to obey like Samuel had done centuries earlier. I shut the Bible and said, "Your servant is here, and I am listening." I sat quietly, not knowing what to expect and still wrapped in my own sad darkness.

Then I heard a voice that I will never forget. I have never been so scared. The sound was so loud that it felt like the whole house was shaking. His majestic voice sounded almost like a roar. He said, *Stop crying and find your strength in Me.*

I was stunned, frightened, and simultaneously elated. For a few moments, I sat in a frozen shock but then jumped up, ran into the bathroom totally charged up, and looked in the mirror. I looked terrible from all the crying, but my eyes were sparkling. I smiled broadly at my reflection. The God of the universe had just taken time out from managing all of creation to come and talk to me. He was real. He was with me. It just blew me away. The might and power of His voice astounded me.

I was aware of a new strength coursing within me and a determined resolve that was not normal. I immediately went downstairs, picked up the phone, called the surgeon's office, and canceled the surgery. God would surely show me the time and the way that I should proceed, but until then, I was not ready. I felt fearless.

CHAPTER 2

And Now for Something Completely Different

There were many day-to-day details and realities that seemed to conspire together to frustrate and steal my hope and joy. Jack had eczema from head to toe, which I was sure made him miserable. Baths and a variety of creams helped, but they did not remove the eczema. Distressed on his behalf, I began to pray about it.

Then the Lord gave me a dream. A young teenager was babysitting Jack, and I came home to find that Jack was totally healed. Excited, I asked, "What did you do?"

She was uncertain, but she said, "I was feeding him these." She showed me a bag of small reddish-brown seeds.

I asked, "What are those?" I had never seen them before.

She said, "Flax seeds."

I woke up and thought, *How clever!* I went to a health-food store and bought flaxseed oil. I started giving him a spoonful each day.

When I told my mother what I was doing, she wisely counseled, "That's not what your dream said. The babysitter said she was feeding Jack the seeds. Why don't you put them in his morning oatmeal?"

A better idea, I thought. So I bought a coffee grinder to make flour from the seeds, which would facilitate adding them to Jack's morning cooked oatmeal. When I went to buy the seeds, I was surprised to find that there were two colors: blond and red-brown. I bought the color that I had seen in the dream. Every day, Jack had a tablespoon of ground flax seeds, which I added to his cooked breakfast cereal. In two weeks, the eczema was gone. Was that a natural solution to Jack's eczema or my faith and obedience to do what the Lord had revealed? It was probably both.

Time passed. Jack's physiotherapist informed me that it was time to get Jack out of his stroller and into a wheelchair, for the sake of his own spine and muscle support. Of course, I had hoped he would be healed and not need it, but that had not happened. So Jack and I went to the clinic at our local rehabilitation hospital so that he could be fitted for a wheelchair.

To my surprise, first, they sent us for a routine hip X-ray. I asked, "Is that really necessary?" Every X-ray was more toxic exposure for him. They assured me it was important.

After that was done, the results were given to his doctor, an orthopedic surgeon, who examined the X-ray and said, "Your son needs hip surgery."

I was shocked. "Why?"

"A ball-and-socket joint on his right hip is actually coming out of joint because of the spasticity of all of his muscles. They're literally pulling his hip out of joint. We will cut all of the tendons around the hip, put the ball back in the socket, perhaps cut the femur (thighbone), and redirect it slightly to reduce the pull."

I was horrified and said, "I assume that means a body cast."

"Yes. Probably six weeks or more." He reassured me that this was a very standard surgery for children with cerebral palsy. He had never seen it reversed without surgery.

I said, "I have to go and pray about it."

He kindly said, "Fine." Then we set up our next appointment.

I went home, informed my husband, and began my quest for healing in prayer with a new determination and alarm. Certainly, I prayed over Jack every morning and evening. Two of the many little booklets that I used were Charles Capps' *The Healing Power of God* and *The Creative Power of God*. These booklets took scriptures and turned them into prayers and declarations that believers could speak out in faith. Many times, I went through the booklets—usually at least two times a day. I was constantly praying.

A couple of months later, I went to the next appointment. This time, my husband came with me. We had another X-ray taken. We then took the pictures to the doctor's clinic. He showed me that it was slightly worse. He said, "That could be due to a camera-angle change, but I do not want to make a big deal about that. I think we need to book the surgery."

I had been praying a lot, and my faith was quite strong because of that. So I said, "Let's make another appointment. I still need to pray."

Then the doctor raised his voice a little, and in a stern

tone, he told me that if I left the situation too long, Jack's hip would come out of joint, which would be very painful for him and make the surgery much harder. He reiterated, "I have never seen this reversed."

I nodded submissively but said, "I must go and pray. I am not ready." With a scowl, he left. My husband looked a little disturbed, but he knew I was not going to be moved on this one.

We went home. Then Bob went to work, Jack lay down for a nap, and I got on my knees and said, *Lord, where are you? I have been praying nonstop—morning, noon, and night. Where are you?* Then unexpectedly, I heard a little whisper on the inside. The Holy Spirit gently said, *Take a nap.* I kind of rolled my eyes in frustration and impatience but obediently lay down and fell asleep.

About five minutes later, I started to wake up. As I left sleep and came into wakefulness, I heard Him say, *Your prayers are not enough.* It was a gentle lightning-bolt revelation. He reminded me that Jesus said, "If two of you agree as on earth concerning anything that they ask, it will be done by my Father in heaven" (Matthew 18:19) I needed to humble myself and actively search for and find people who could agree with me in prayer. A lukewarm, "Oh, sure, I'll pray with you, Laurel," would not do. What I required was believers who would and could join their faith for healing with my faith for healing. Not very many people that I knew could do that.

As it happened, the next night Benny Hinn was in town. I drove another one of my spiritual mothers, Billie, down to the crusade. We parked and entered Maple Leaf Gardens. During one of the intermissions, we went out for a little break, and I told her what had happened.

She said, "Perfect! My husband was just diagnosed with prostate cancer. We are going to pray right now that none of these medical proclamations will happen but that he will, in fact, be healed." So together there at a sticky little hot-dog condiments bar outside the main part of the arena, we prayed. I knew things were going to begin to move.

As an aside, her husband was completely healed of cancer. He lived many more years until he died suddenly of heart failure, which had nothing to do with the cancer. Other people who joined with me in prayer were parents of other children who had problems, as well as my friends Elaine and her son Conor. They had spent a lot of time with Jack and me, and they loved us, so they joined us to pray for Jack's hip to be healed.

I knew that most of my family was not ready to pray that prayer, although I did enlist prayers from his brothers when it seemed appropriate. A scripture that I found and used daily was from Hebrews 12:12–13.

> Therefore, strengthen the hands that hang down and the feeble knees and make straight paths for your feet, so that what is lame may not be dislocated but rather be healed.

The next time we went back to the doctor, we got the prerequisite X-ray, and he put it up on the light box. Even he was surprised. Jack's hip joint was looking a little bit better. He looked at me quizzically and said, "What have you been doing?"

"Praying," I said.

He continued to search. "Are you doing any new physiotherapy?"

"No," I said. "In fact, I have dropped some exercise protocols because they're not doing any good, and they are a lot of work for me."

He said, "So nothing different?"

"No." We agreed to have another follow-up visit in a couple months.

The Word of God says, "Beloved, do not cast away your confidence, which has a great reward. For you have need of endurance, so that after you have done the will of God, you may receive the promise" (Hebrews 10:35–36).

At each visit for the next five years, every X-ray showed improvement. It was a long haul, but we reached the desired end. At that time, the resident physician, who thought the whole thing was weird, would not come into the room. But the nice Jewish orthopedic surgeon smiled and said, "His hip looks great. Keep doing whatever it is you are doing. If you need me, call me. But I do not see any reason to pursue these visits any longer."

Hallelujah! Even though it took five years, this was a living example of Mark 11:22–24, which says, "Jesus answered and said to them, 'Have faith in God. For assuredly I say to you, whosoever says to the mountain, "Be removed and be cast in to the sea" and does not doubt in his heart, but believes that those things he says will be done, he will have whatever he says.'"

I had experienced a major victory in the healing of Jack's hip, but perhaps then, I had become self-satisfied and lowered my guard. Obviously I was a committed seeker of truth. However, you can be in the kingdom and still be pulled off course. I was still very much a product of the 1960s North American music and media culture.

As a child, I had believed in Jesus, but our family's

church attendance had only lasted a few years. During middle school, I became a feminist, largely because of my mother's influence. I began reading new-age books, followed pictures and explanations of yoga exercises, and tried meditations based on several authors' instructions. I also became interested in the paranormal and occult world. I was a seeker, but I was busily running down the wrong paths.

When we had our first child, I took an online university course on world religions. I wanted to know what the truth was. I wrote an A+ paper on Hinduism, its temple architecture, and its worship. But none of these studies helped me at all. In fact, they added to my confusion. I realized that each religion had some virtue and general truth that attracted followers, but I wanted *the* truth and *the* way—something that really worked.

I had repented of my earlier pagan forays and turned fully toward Christianity, but I soon realized that I was still vulnerable to certain ungodly drawings and pulls. The following is one life-altering example.

When Jack was still very young, I had arranged for a piano teacher to come to the house and give lessons to his three older brothers. The teacher was also a vocalist at a large downtown church and a born-again Christian. We became friends. Knowing of my desire to bring healing to Jack and our family, she told me about a man in the church who was giving courses on spirituality. While she recommended him to me, she cautioned that she herself had not gone to the course, but others had said that they really enjoyed his insights.

At great expense, I called the man and booked what he called a "counseling session." In our session, the first thing that disturbed me was that he invoked the names of many religious gods that I knew from my world religions' course. He called on Buddha, Shiva, some first-nations' gods, Jesus, and Jehovah. The list seemed long. I left thinking that the session was interesting and because he had been recommended by a Christian, I overlooked the odd beginning of our session and hoped his insights would be helpful.

The next time I went to see him, he told me that he wanted me to go and see another gifted visionary that he respected. *A prophet?* I wondered. I made an appointment as he had suggested.

I went to meet this second counselor. Before I attended this session, I had had a dream. In my dream I was a detective trying to solve a mystery with a handful of friends. There was a very strange situation. People were seemingly disappearing without a trace. We went to see if we could solve the mystery, which was occurring inside a particular office building that was now deserted, due to everyone's fear.

All of the office furniture had been removed from the floor we were on. Only permanent walls and cubicle dividers remained in this ghost-town office. I was aware that we were very high up in the building. I could see beyond the office partitions that there were big glass floor-to-ceiling windows.

It was a foggy day, so I could not see anything outside but a yellow-gray colored wall of atmospheric sludge. I noted a fireplace, which was just inside the entrance of the office. It appeared neat, tidy, and unused. Strangely, two Chinese dog statues, which were about two feet high, sat on either side of the fire grate. Coming from the middle of the modern concrete fireplace opening, there was a very strange, curvy path, which was made out of strips of kindling. They were about an inch-and-a-half wide, eight inches long, and a quarter of an inch thick.

I thought, *What is that doing there?* I walked to the window, wondering about this and trying to see through the fog. I turned slowly to leave the building while still pondering it.

All of a sudden, I heard a loud whooshing sound, turned, and saw a fire rush out of the two dogs' mouths. The flames instantly ignited the kindling, and a raging wall of fire, which was the height of the ceiling and about four feet wide, raced along the path of the kindling and ended at the window.

In a flash, I realized that the people who had disappeared had either been instantly incinerated or had jumped through the window to their deaths. Clearly all had been incinerated because the windows were still intact. This solved the mystery of the disappearing people. I woke up, felt totally alarmed, but was not sure how to pray. I prayed protection for everyone that I knew and loved until I finally fell asleep again.

A few days later, I went to my scheduled appointment for spiritual counseling. A gracious and attractive young man offered me lemonade and a seat in a living room where I could wait. I sat down, and to my horror, the fireplace had two Chinese dogs that were exactly like the ones in my dream. I realize now that I was still so insecure in my faith that I did not have the nerve to run. I sat stunned.

Today, I believe that I would have left. That moment as I pondered the weirdness of the situation, I was called upstairs to my appointment. Feeling very alarmed, I threw up a flash prayer: *God, if I am not supposed to be here, I'm sorry. Protect me and let me just leave.* I found out later that the man that I had visited was a medium and a channeler. He supposedly gave messages from a dead spirit who spoke through him.

I completely shut down within my soul. I cannot remember a word that he said. I just wanted to leave. When he asked me if I had any questions, I said, "No, thank you. Goodbye." I had been so polite, but I remained confused.

Afterward, I asked the Lord what I should do other than repent and ask for cleansing. I felt that He told me to go back to the first counselor and tell him my dream— how the exact duplicate dogs had been in the channeler's home— and how I felt. He said that I should pay for his time before I ended contact with him. It was a warning from the Lord.

I did go back to the first counselor who had recommended the channeler and shared my dream, my visit, and the fire-breathing Chinese dogs. It was as if I could see a mask falling from his face and a little glimmer of fear arising in his eyes. It is good, healthy, and wise to fear the Lord. I left feeling that I had learned my lesson. I had been obedient to deliver the Lord's message. I prayed that the counselor would receive it. It was now between him and God to make things right.

Thus corrected and protected, I was even more determined to follow only biblical precepts, the Holy Spirit, and people that I trusted. I continued to worship, pray, and study within my women's Christian group and at the church. I was now reading the Bible faithfully, having purchased the *Bible in a Year* as a reading guide. I was still journaling. I would first spend some time in the Lord's presence, pray, and then ask the Holy Spirit for scriptures to look up. I would jot down the references. Later, I would look them up, write them down, and journal about them. The Lord would talk to me through His Word. It was often frighteningly relevant but always very helpful.

CHAPTER 3

The Toronto Blessing

It was the spring of 1994. The women who were discipling me took me to a women's Saturday meeting at the new 'Toronto Blessing' Fellowship. Many seasoned and mature Christians were excited about the unusual and powerful manifestation and outpouring of the Holy Spirit, which began in January of 1994. John and Carol Arnott pastored this church formally called the Toronto Airport Christian Fellowship. Spirit-filled Christians from around the world began to come to experience the touch of God. I don't remember much about the women's meeting that I went to except that it was encouraging.

A few months later, we learned that this church was hosting their first healing conference in October. I wanted to go. I wondered if I could arrange it. A friend went to sign up and insisted that they accept her application in advance on my behalf because I had a disabled baby at home and could not be there to sign up myself. God bless her determination.

I was still nursing Jack, but I had help during the day at that stage, so I was able to juggle family needs and still attend the conference. I would nurse Jack, drive half an hour to the 10:00 a.m. meeting near the airport, drive home at lunchtime, nurse him again, drive back for the afternoon meeting, drive home, nurse him, get him and the kids to bed, and drive back out again for the evening service. I returned home at around 1:00 a.m. I repeated that for three days. What had seemed to be a daunting task was, in fact, a remarkable experience.

There were probably four thousand people in the huge ballroom at the Constellation Hotel, complete with its sparking chandeliers, reflective walls, and comfortable, padded chairs. I was sitting with my mentors when for the first time, I saw a particularly awesome manifestation of the Holy Spirit. It looked as if the Holy Spirit was wind blowing through a field of tall ripened wheat. Anywhere from one-to-three-people deep, this wind-like presence would blow through the room. It was obvious where it was moving. Any person it touched any place in its path either fell off her chair (being slain in the Spirit) or started laughing hilariously in what they called holy laughter. There was definitely a powerful impact!

I could see it coming toward us. As it went by, some of my women friends were touched and laughed, shook, or fell. Nothing happened to me. I was so disappointed.

The next morning as I drove in, it was with some trepidation. I really did not want to be the one person who was not touched by the Holy Spirit. I had felt so rejected in earlier meetings, and I wondered if I was just too depressed, distracted, or worldly to be able to laugh.

Sure enough during the morning meeting, the wind of the Spirit started to move. As He came our way, my heart sank, and I thought, *Oh, no.* However, as it passed by, I illogically and uncontrollably started to laugh from the depths of my belly and roll on the floor. It was both ridiculous and glorious. It felt like He was saying to me, *Your grief and pain are not bigger than Me, and I see you.* How liberating it was! That was an important transition for me.

At the conference, the head of the women's ministry, Mary Audrey Raycroft, announced that her Gifts of the Holy Spirit class was starting on Wednesday nights in October, and I was determined to attend them, and I did. Of course, I wanted to know about the gift of healing. I kept asking about it in each class, and she kept telling me to wait. There were nine gifts of the Holy Spirit listed in 1 Corinthians 12. We spent some time learning about the gift of tongues, interpretation, prophecy, words of wisdom, and so on. I waited.

I did not know that they sometimes all worked together. Her class became not only instructive but also another open door. One night, she remarked that some people wanted to run around healing everybody while their spouses were not saved. I sat there and thought, *Whoops! That is probably me.*

I went to speak with her after the class. She sent me over to the man who headed up their New Life Salvation team, Gary Patton. He spent some time with me and gave me some detailed instructions. "For one week every day, declare out loud these scriptures in your house. Remember, you are using your authority given to you as a believer in Jesus Christ."

I looked up the scriptures that he recommended. They demanded that demons be bound, forbid their operation or interference, and reminded them of the words in the Bible and the authority of Jesus Christ.

The following week again in the house, I was to vocally declare kingdom-building scriptures, welcome in the Holy Spirit, and ask Him to bring His presence and salvation to the household. Then, he instructed, "Ask the Holy Spirit for the time that He has appointed for you to speak with your husband. You can then ask him if he wants to hear the gospel and wants to be born again. When he says yes, read this little Billy Graham booklet. Don't add anything. Don't take anything out. Get him to sign it and then do what husbands and wives do in a blessed marital covenant!"

I did all of it. Three weeks later at class, I happily announced that it had worked. The two leaders seemed stunned. I was surprised that they were surprised, but I realized my childlike expectation, faith, and obedience had accomplished the desired result. God had already been faithful to answer my prayers, and I had fully expected Him to bless my obedience in this. God does reward those who diligently seek Him.

As a bonus, I was asked to join the New Life Salvation team. That was a privilege. Every Tuesday night, I helped pray for people who came forward for salvation and ministry. I really enjoyed it.

As the Gifts of the Holy Spirit classes progressed, I was encouraged to join the ministry team, which prayed for all the people who attended the meetings. I chose Wednesday nights to be on the team. I became very good at getting the children to bed early, rushing out, and driving to the church, singing and praying as I went.

At one stage, my husband was annoyed and said, "You're spending too much time at church."

My response was, "You can have me depressed or at church," so life went on as it had. I fulfilled my family duties, and I was encouraged and greatly strengthened during the worship and church ministry time. I would be charged up with energy and hope, which completely offset the 1:00–2:00 a.m. return home and my reduced sleep.

The first night that I was on the ministry team, I wondered if anything would happen. I so wanted to be a vessel that the Holy Spirit could use to bless others. Another woman was assigned to instruct, pray with, and generally oversee me. I thought the arrangement would go on for some time. My training only lasted one night.

Now on my own, I was nervous, but the Holy Spirit was faithful. I started to realize His touch had very little to do with me. His grace truly was sufficient for the ministry time. He was within me but also everywhere in the building. His desire was to meet His people, love them, bless them, and heal them.

Meanwhile, our family's home life continued. Over the years, Elaine and Conor had started coming over once or twice a week to take Jack for a walk and play with him on the floor. He loved their visits, silly games, and prayers. He especially loved it when we all sang together, in praise and worship, and with Elaine on the guitar. She would often pause and wait for Jack to loudly vocalize his part in the songs. He was fully engaged. Sometimes I would also go on walks with them. Sometimes I would get other things done or just take a break. He loved their visits.

We all developed a very close bond and quickly learned that the only controlled sound that Jack could make was the sound of a kiss. This smacking kiss became his "Yes," "Amen," and "I love you." It was very useful. It became obvious that he had opinions and that his brain was working pretty well.

Our eldest son had become very involved in the youth group at the church. When he was fifteen and at a youth conference, he witnessed his friend's younger sister manifesting a demon, flailing, shrieking, and then subsequently settling into a peaceful calm of the Holy Spirit's deliverance. Our son was alarmed but somewhat gratified that the Bible was true. He enjoyed telling me all about his initial horror and the Lord's healing resolution.

He agreed to my going with him to their youth meetings every Friday night. I drove to the youth meetings, sat in the back of the room, quietly observed, and prayed. I interceded for the young people and their leaders. I also did my best to stay out of their way and be unobtrusive. They learned and had a lot of fun. I found myself wishing that I could have had this kind of oasis in my youth. I prayed that the Lord would raise up leaders so that more youth would find a similar group for themselves. Afterward, I often drove a carload of teenagers to the post-meeting social time at the local Tim Hortons coffee shop. Deep friendships and faith were growing.

I vividly remember when they finally had their first youth-only conference on an Easter weekend. I was happy to drive some of the participants there. Then I went upstairs to the balcony to pray for the sea of well over one thousand young people. Some were with their group leaders or parents. They looked like a living, moving tapestry as they sat on the floor or milled about because the chairs had been removed from the sanctuary.

The youth pastor came to the microphone and said, "Let's all stand up and worship the Lord." In a few moments, they all turned their attention on him, stood, and faced the worship team on the platform. The first notes cut through the atmosphere, riveting their attention. I could feel a wave of power commingling with the loud worship music and rushing out over them. It came toward me and even went up into the balcony. I started to weep. I could feel the pleasure and power of the Holy Spirit in that place.

God desires to minister powerfully to our young people. If we will make church a priority, He will visit our youth, bring hope, and restore a sense of significance and destiny.

Years later, our second and third sons joined the youth group for a while, but unfortunately, their much-loved leader was replaced, and they refused to go back. Teens can be stubborn. Convincing them to go to church on Sundays became a real chore. Our eldest son had gone to university at that point, and after months of continued discord, our second son also went to university. I was left with our third son, who still did not want to go to church.

Exasperated, I went to the Lord and said, *What do I do?* Sometimes your best answers to prayer come when you don't really expect an answer.

I heard the Lord say, *Home-church him*. I had heard of homeschooling. I had never heard of home-churching, but I thought it was a good idea. I consulted with my husband and then offered our son a proposal. He would either go to church with us (a two-hour service) or give me his undivided attention—without any attitude—for half an hour at home. He chose the latter (surprise, surprise). Every Sunday, I could feel his soul shift. It was a very rewarding time.

Meanwhile Jack and his dad were going to the big church. About a year later, our third son went to university as well. My husband said, "How about you home-church Jack, and I will be able to enjoy church myself." That seemed fair to me because I was still going to church every Wednesday night as well as conferences and special events. As it turned out, Jack had started to make his displeasure about going to church known by being noisy, kind of squawky, and generally impatient. He did not like people coming up to and praying for him. Sometimes they even laid hands on him without asking. This is a lesson for us all.

In an effort to satisfy everyone, I asked Elaine if she and her son Conor would consider joining Jack and me in our home church. They were delighted. A high school friend of Conor's, who was an international student from southern China, came as well. He had never seen a disabled child. He was the *one child* that his parents were allowed to have, within the one-child policy of communist China. Disabled children would not be allowed to remain alive. Jack and this young man became very good friends. Jack actually helped him find his future wife, but that's another story. Week by week, our little congregation would worship, hear a little reading from the Bible, and pray. We really enjoyed one another and the presence of the Lord.

Because I had joined the ministry team, I started their training to pray for individual attendees during ministry time. I had taken the Gifts of the Holy Spirit class and joined the New Life team. I instructed new believers and helped them understand who they were as new creations in Christ. Additionally, every time I was at the church, I heard some of the best teaching and preaching that was available in North America because these leaders wanted to come, minister under, and experience the powerful anointing that was present in the church. I still went to our little Wednesday Bible study. I was teachable, hungry, and desperately seeking more understanding of what it was to be a Christian and the privileges and responsibilities thereof.

Increasingly, members of the church's congregation were being released into powerful ministry. For example, there were two women from our church, whom I really respected as intercessors, who offered a free journaling seminar. Joanne and Shirley first led us in worship and then spoke about spiritual disciplines, the scriptures, and the desire of the Father to communicate with His children.

Shirley told us how the Lord had asked her to make a floral wedding crown for ministry. God would anoint their teaching on journaling and attendee participation. After ministry, she was to lay the bridal crown on the head of every participant at the seminar. The Lord wanted to impart a revelation to each attendee of himself or herself as the bride of Christ. It was to be placed on everyone, whether you were a male or a female. The crown was a very pretty, circular, flowered wreath with ribbons hanging down the back.

We practiced journaling, and in small groups, we began to share the things that the Lord had said to us. In turn, each person would read from his or her journal. We could all see that it was from the Lord and very anointed. Some wept as they were deeply touched. Then we were invited to stand in a line across the front of the room and enter into the Lord's presence as we listened to worship music. We waited for our turn to receive the wreath on our heads. The atmosphere was relaxed but expectant, and the worship music was very calming.

As I stood with my eyes closed and my hands lifted in a relaxed way (palms up in surrender), I suddenly had a vision. It looked like I was inside the vestibule of St. Paul's Cathedral in London, England, but the sanctuary was completely empty of congregants and pews. I could see the imposing architecture, beautiful windows, pillars, and tiled, black-and-white floor.

Father God appeared as a huge fiery orb of light on the raised platform. Jesus stood on the main floor just in front of Him. I was in a very elaborate and expensive wedding dress. I looked a lot like Lady Diana in her glorious wedding gown. It's the kind of dress I would never, in the natural, have chosen—never! Jesus came toward me, greeted me at the doorway, smiled sweetly, and proceeded to walk me down the aisle. As I approached the Father, the music on the CD recording sounded like ringing church bells.

Only God could orchestrate the timing, and in the vision, I knew that the Father was receiving and approving of me. He then motioned and pointed to his right, indicating that I was to sit on the bridal bench. Jesus was to be at His right hand, and I was seated next to Jesus.

I could feel my heart change as the ministry wreath was then placed on my head. I was completely enveloped in a love and honor that was supernatural. I understood myself to be His bride. My identity was transformed. I realized that He wanted us all to enter the romance and security of our place as His bride. We were deeply loved and cherished. Revelations like this lift us to new levels of faith and security.

A few months later, I dreamed of a beautiful beach

house. It was a modern-looking bungalow with a lot of big glass windows. It sat near a sandy, white beach. It reminded me of the windswept beaches that I had seen in pictures of Cape Cod. I knew it was my house. I could see the blue, sparkling water.

I walked toward the sprawling, modern, but earthy bungalow of glass, decks, and wood. I then opened the door and walked inside, expecting it to be just as gorgeous inside as it was from the outside, but instead, I was shocked. To my horror, there were demons of all shapes, colors, and sizes everywhere. Some looked like they were human, but most did not. I stood and surveyed the situation. I was surprisingly unafraid but wondered what I should do. After all, they were uninvited and loitering in my beautiful house.

At that moment, one of the little imps pointed a finger at me. Immediately and at the same exact moment, the muscles in the middle of my back went into painful spasms. I could feel the familiar pain in my dream. This spasm was something that had happened fairly regularly to me since I was about seventeen. I can now recall that this all started after beginning yoga. Was it a coincidence? I don't think so. In the dream, I was outraged and told the little demon, "Stop that!" He gave me an impish smile and pointed at me. Again, my back had a spasm. I knew with certainty that this demon was responsible for the spasms that had afflicted my body.

In my frustration, I looked to the one who seemed to be the leader and said, "Tell him to stop that!" He gave me a mocking look, shrugged his shoulders, and turned away, as if so say, "Who cares?" The imp did it again, and this time, I said more assertively, "In the name of Jesus Christ, you stop that right now!" Poof! He disappeared.

Every eyeball in the room slowly turned and focused on me in fear and trepidation. The leader, who was now much more ingratiating, cautiously said to me, "You are not going to do that again, are you?"

As I woke up, I got the message. Jesus had given me authority to use His name. I knew it from the Word of God (see Luke 10:19 and John 14:13). It had never occurred to me that I could apply it so simply and get such a dramatic result. I was on a new trajectory and began to apply my newfound authority whenever I could. By the way, that chronic back spasm and weak muscle pain never returned, even after twenty-five years of it happening frequently (especially in pregnancy and the early years of motherhood).

My ministry training was accelerating. Be it scripture, church history, or ministerial books, I was diligent in all of my reading. I daily repented of any personal, family, national, and religious sins that came to mind. Our church began to engage in an intensive prayer ministry for deliverance and cleansing from men's involvement in Freemasonry in their family lines.

I had heard my mother proudly talking about her grandfather being awarded the honorary Freemasonry level of the Scottish Rite, but I did not know what that meant, and I doubt she did either. This much-loved academic grandfather had unknowingly opened the gates of hell to his generations. Before I went into the session, the Holy Spirit prompted me to phone my mother-in-law, and to my surprise, her father had been in a high position within the Masonic organization. She also told me that my father-in-law's father had also joined the first level, but he did not attend for very long. This information was revealed with a hint of pride in the association. My own father had been abandoned as a child, so I did not know about his family line, but I now knew that at least three of the four family bloodlines were tainted with this satanic organization.

All through the afternoon ministry time and as we broke each oath, I could think of someone in our family who had been afflicted with a corresponding curse or physical infirmity. This was because with each spoken oath, the novice had also read a corresponding punishment that had been inflicted if someone revealed any of the Masonic secrets or broke the oath in any way. The irony is that even though participants might have tried to keep the secrets and the oath, the curses manifested anyway. It was such a diabolical deception. Almost everyone in the ministry room experienced some manifestation in their emotions or body, which indicated that the deliverance was real.

Not long afterward on a day and time when I was not doing anything in particular, the Holy Spirit once again graciously brought me a vision of my beach house. I felt that He directed me to look inside once more. The house was now tidy, clean, bright, and tastefully furnished. Most importantly, it was completely free of demons. Hallelujah in Jesus's name! My holy husband, Jesus, had given me a new home and shown me that the temple of my body, which the house represented, was now in order and ready for use.

CHAPTER 4

Personal Ministry and Taking Responsibility

Every night at the church, when we felt our own individual team ministry time was finished, we were instructed to pray with another team member to be cleaned off spiritually and refilled before we left for home. One night, it was really late, and not very many team members were left. There were always many attendees who wanted and waited for prayer.

I finally found a woman on the team who had a moment to pray for me. I had always thought she was really odd. As I knelt down on the floor, I asked, "Could you just give me a quick prayer so I can go home?" She was happy to do that, and she launched into a lovely prayer. As she put her hand on my head, I could feel a stream of what felt like warm maple syrup going down through my body. The Holy Spirit said to me, *Don't ever judge one of my servants again.* Smack! I understood that I had been too quick to judge her as 'odd' while the Lord clearly loved and had anointed her.

As time went on, the ministry team was asked to attend a one-week training by John and Paula Sanford, who were from Elijah House. I had never heard of them. I did not see how I could manage five days away from home to attend summer school. The woman that I had judged earlier was very distressed. Inquiring, I learned that she wanted to attend but that she did not have money for the tuition.

With a repentant heart I said, "You go for me. I'll pay your tuition." She was thrilled. Then she paused and asked me why I was not going. I explained that I had four children—one with a lot of issues—who were all home for summer vacation. It was not possible unless my husband took a week off work. I could not see that happening.

She then launched into prayer that he would want to do this and that it would all work out so that I could attend as well. With a glimmer of hope and some trepidation, I went home and laid out the school program for my husband. My plan did not get a very warm reception. However, the next day, my husband came back with a better plan. We would have our daytime help stay in the house for the five days with Jack while I was doing my daytime class, and my husband would take the three older brothers on a train trip to Agawa Canyon. *Perfect!* I thought. We were all content. I enrolled in the Elijah House Week-One School, and it became a doorway to a whole new era in my life.

As the class began, we started learning about inner healing and prayer counseling. There were seventy to eighty participants. Mostly pastors and seasoned Christians were taking the course. On the first day, John Sanford announced that they needed three guinea pigs to be counseled in front of everyone on each of the next three days. The Sandfords would demonstrate how prayer counseling was done. The bad news was that you had to divulge the details and sin in your life. The good news was that you had seventy intercessors in the room and a really good chance for a major healing from the Lord.

The Holy Spirit said to me, *You could do that. You don't really know anybody here, right?* So I submitted my name. The next morning, John announced that he and his wife had a very clear direction from the Lord. They had picked the names. He said, "I am not sure who this is, but Laurel, where are you?" My heart sank, and I was elated at the same time when he said, "You are on today after lunch."

Normally I am a pretty chatty, social person, but I could not sit or talk with anyone. Feeling miserable and inexplicably antisocial, I took my lunch outside to the parking lot and ate it while sitting in the grass. I muttered out loud, "I feel like a weed in the garden of life."

The Holy Spirit said, *Look.* I looked down at my feet, and there were lots of little wildflowers. There were little snapdragon-like flowers and all kinds of other ones. A little sapling was a few feet away, and all of a sudden, it was filled with at least twenty kinds of little birds, which were all happily chirping as birds do. I knew that He was saying supernaturally, *You are okay. I am here.* So I went back up and divulged my life as they asked questions.

"Were you wanted?"

I laughed. "None of us were wanted. We happened." All kinds of questions followed. Finally, they led me in a prayer of repentance and knelt down on either side of my chair, locking arms behind my back.

John, who was very prophetic, announced, "You have never sat between mother-father love."

I said, "I don't know if I ever sat with either parent with

their arm around me." At that moment, I felt enveloped by the Sandford's love.

When they finished praying, I was shaking from head to toe. As I returned to my seat, a pastor's wife from Hamilton sat beside and put her arm around me. She said, "I think you need some company." She was so right. I was still shaking.

At the end of the day, I drove home, fed Jack, put him to bed, and lay down in my bed. Every muscle in my body hurt. It reminded me of the way that I had felt after being in a car accident and the jarring, tense, and aching muscle response. As I lay there with some worship music on over the next four hours or so, all the pain seemed to drain into the mattress. At four in the morning, I was ready to go dancing. I felt fantastic. My body had released so much of life's tensions and traumas, which had somehow been trapped within me.

Deliverance and inner healing has a profound manifestation within our physical beings. A whole new kind of peace and joy had taken up residence. I asked the Lord how I could bless the Sandfords because I felt so grateful and blessed. The Holy Spirit showed me two things. I would take a clean sheet, two pillows, and some nice body cream and have the ministry team massage and anoint their hands and feet while they were relaxing and lying on the floor. He indicated, *They are tired, and this would bless them.*

I thought, *I could do that.* Determined, I gathered up all the things that I believed He had suggested.

Then He said, *You have ten thousand dollars in a savings' account. I want you to take it out and give it to them.* I always considered that money as my emergency fund. I had saved it when I had been working full-time. I realized that He was saying, *Give me your security blanket.*

After very little sleep but feeling happily renewed, I went back to the church and asked if anyone wanted to help me with the anointing. Several well-meaning Christians thought that the idea was too new-age sounding and perhaps not right. So I asked John Sanford what he thought.

He smiled and said, "That sounds lovely." As for the ten thousand dollars, it would take time to get a check, so that was delivered on the last day of the school. The Holy Spirit's directives had been accomplished.

I'd like to say that life was immediately wonderful, but that is not quite what happened. Sometimes the monotony of life just seemed to roll along. But several months later, I got a letter in the mail from John Sandford, telling me that the Lord had told him that I needed encouragement. He wanted to provide me with some context.

He had overspent while building a playground for his grandchildren, hosting several pastors' families, and taking them to Yosemite Park and the Old Faithful geyser. He had said to the Lord, "If You will give me ten thousand dollars, I will pay my debt and not do this again." Then he said, "Laurel, God used you to answer my prayer. I am very grateful." You can imagine how I was both blessed and encouraged by this wonderful man of God. I had heard the Lord's instructions correctly and obeyed.

Fall turned into winter, and I think my husband was starting to feel somewhat guilty about all the family trips and weekend skiing time that he and three of our sons were enjoying while I stayed at home with Jack. I did not resent this family dynamic. I wanted our sons to have as full a life as possible. An opportunity came up to go with our third son's choir to sing in England. Bob suggested that I go as a chaperone. I was thrilled.

I am not sure that our twelve-year-old son was so happy, but off we went with the school choir. We stayed at a YMCA and had an excellent tour guide who had been a choir boy in his youth in Canterbury Cathedral. Before he retired and became a guide, he had been a policeman in London. He was a wealth of information and very good with the boys.

I had my own room at the YMCA. I was mostly left on my own during the day, as the boys came and went in little packs. The few teachers that had come kept to themselves, and the other two mothers were friends. I actually enjoyed being alone. I felt that the Holy Spirit was very close during the whole trip. I reveled in the beauty of the country and historic buildings as the boys' choir sang beautiful Christian songs in some of the finest churches and cathedrals in England. I lit candles, said prayers, and enjoyed it all. When we went up in the London Eye, which is a Ferris wheel, it was an exciting time to ponder God looking down on a city.

I prayed. No matter what your circumstance is, the Holy Spirit is available, willing, and able to fill us with His joy and peace. I think that He really enjoys leading us into adventures that are big and small.

On one of our days of touring, we went to the Tower of London. We stood in a very long line of tourists who were waiting to see the crown jewels. I was shepherding at the back end of our group and essentially alone. As I got closer to the building, I could feel an anointing come upon me, and I wondered why it was happening. Then I started to cry. I was surprised. I was not consciously sad in any way. I wondered what the Holy Spirit wanted to show me.

As I got closer to the building, I could see a large overhead screen with a video on it that was in a loop. It was footage of Queen Elizabeth II arriving for her coronation at Westminster Abbey. The crowd celebrated as she arrived. Once she was inside the abbey, we all watched her receiving her royal mantle, the scepter, the orb, and the crown. A group of men were standing behind her in a semicircle and helping her with the process. I watched as tears streamed down my face. I wondered what was going on within me.

The Holy Spirit then whispered to me, *That's you!*

I said, *No, Lord.* I could just as easily have said, *Get behind me Satan.* It all seemed ridiculous.

I heard the Holy Spirit again say, *Laurel, that is you.*

No, Lord.

Then in a tone that sounded a little angry, He said, *That's you, and if you can't accept that, I can't use you.* That startled me. I repented for what had now been revealed to me as my arrogant assumptions of the way that humility looked and a large dose of my insecurities. I was stunned.

Then I pondered. *Ah,* I remembered, *the royal priesthood.* The authority given to us by Jesus through His name was a revelation that was shaking the foundations of the way that I saw myself compared with the way that He saw me. This revelation was a *wow* bequest.

We moved onward and saw the exhibit of the mantle, the scepter, the jeweled orb, magnificent cups, and other items that they used in the coronation. They were highlighting the jewels, their expense, and especially their weight. Gold, silver, and jewels are heavy. I realized that the men who were helping the new queen were, in many ways, like intercessors helping her to carry the physical weight of the emblems of her office, as well as the spiritual and governmental weight. She needed their assistance. Again, I realized how important it was to know the Word and now specifically, to know that New Testament believers were royal priests in Christ Jesus. As we mature spiritually, we are empowered and anointed to intercede, rule and co-labour with the King of kings, according to His Word and will and in His name. What a privilege and honour!

Receiving prayer counseling early in my Christian walk had been important. It's something I would recommend to anyone desiring an accelerated result in his or her faith walk. Let me add that there always seems to be more the Holy Spirit wants to reveal, heal and illuminate.

Later on, a girlfriend in the church was convinced that like her, I had been sexually abused as a little girl, even though I could not remember it. I knew that trauma was often repressed. Her thinking was that my young adult promiscuity had probably been related to that. She was going to a counselor in a nearby town, and she recommended that I go.

I really did not want to spend the time or the money. I was praying about it because she kept bringing it up. Finally, I asked, *Lord, do you want me to go?*

I felt that He said, *Are you afraid?*

I thought about it. Maybe I was a little bit afraid. Taking on a new resolve and courage, I acquiesced and agreed to go. I did not want to live in fear. My desire was to be a woman of faith.

As our session began, the husband-wife team instructed

me to ask the Holy Spirit for an inner picture of a safe place for the duration of the counseling. The thing that immediately came to mind was a huge Jesus who laid me in the palm of His hand and tucked me into the gap made by the piercing of His side. Then He laid his hand over that space. It was as if I were lying in a little hammock, resting, protected, and close to His heart. It was a lovely and safe place.

We then did a lot of prayer work concerning my maternal family and line: the broken marriages, the frustrated, intelligent women, and other events that were both good and the bad. It was revealed that I had harshly judged my mother as a little girl. At parties in our home, I had seen her flirting seductively with other men a few times. In my childish simplicity, I was offended for my father's sake. I doubt that anybody else thought anything of it. It was adult behavior, but I did not understand that, and I did not like it. I guess that I thought I was somehow protecting my father.

The Bible's fifth commandment (taken from the Ten Commandments) is the first one that addresses human relationships. It specifically instructs us to honor our mother and father. The promise is that we will live long and inherit the land. We will prosper. Jesus later tells us not to judge so that we will not be judged. Similarly with the measure we use for others, it will be measured back to us.

All through the Bible, there is the law of increase. Everything increases, for good or for evil. For example, good seeds produce flowers, vegetables, and trees. Bad seeds produce weeds. When combining those three laws in my case—dishonoring my mother, judging my mother, and the law of increase on my sin, at a very early age—I manifested the feminine seductive charm that I had judged my mother for. I think by the time I was twelve, I was very flirtatious. As you can imagine, it quickly led me into a lot of trouble. That dynamic became a ministry focus.

At the end of the ministry counseling, I had a vision of a gigantic cruise ship in dry dock. Oddly, it was already full of people cheering and celebrating. Confetti was floating everywhere. There was the smashing of champagne bottles and the cutting of the ribbon. Then the ship was launched into the water. It was a very joyful scene, and somehow, I realized that something major had just happened. I believe that I was set free from a maternal lineage of sinful seduction. Now the way was open for a new level of life and ministry as a woman.

The spirit of seduction seen by my girlfriend had been rooted in my maternal line. This spirit attracted all the wrong kinds of people to me, and the wrong kind of attention. That root needed to be and was removed.

My lessons in prayer counseling with Elijah House and the Sandfords continued with the church ministry team as my hunger to know the Lord and live for Him increased. I enjoyed all the teaching and training, and I was eager to apply it to myself. I was very busy cleaning up my life. I desired to offload my self-condemnation and insecurities and to be healed and at peace.

One morning in our Elijah House training session, I felt unusually empty and flat. I sat listening to the morning teaching and wondered why. I had already learned that anything out of the ordinary might well be the Holy Spirit trying to get my attention and revealing something to me. That was exactly what was happening. They announced that the morning teaching was on the sin of abortion. My heart sank a bit. I had not addressed this area of my life.

When I was fifteen, I found the person that I thought was the love of my life—my first serious boyfriend. I adored him. It's funny how at fifteen, I could easily be convinced that this was the one that I should marry. Kissing, hugging, talking, and being close were all part of our relationship. He began to press me more and more for sexual intimacy. In my desire to please him, I began to succumb to the pressure. Our involvement slowly became more sexual, as the passions of young love drove our relationship. To my horror, I became pregnant.

At the time, I prayed the best way that I knew how. I learned "The Lord's Prayer" at school, and it was all that I knew. I searched the *Yellow Pages* for a phone number and address of a family doctor that I could reach by bus, to determine whether my suspicions were accurate. He confirmed my fears. He was very kind and sympathetic. He told me that he knew of a doctor in a Toronto hospital who performed legal abortions. He would contact him for me. When that was accomplished, my boyfriend and I attended our scheduled appointment. We were informed that because I was only fifteen, I needed parental consent for the surgical procedure. I felt like there was an earthquake inside me.

Alone at home with my distress, I pondered the enormity of the situation. I felt the burden, heaviness, and shame of being a huge disappointment to my parents. My mother had repeatedly warned all four of her daughters about the dangerous realities of early pregnancy. She herself had conceived a child in high school, which had become the urgent driving force for a speedy wedding ceremony. Several times in my fear and shame, I lay in the bathtub thinking about how easy it would be to just go under the water and breathe it in. I did not have the strength to do it.

My mother told me later that when she learned of my pregnancy and scheduled abortion, she took the dog for a walk in a nearby ravine and cried and cried. She realized I had stepped into something that she understood. Despite all of her counsel and warnings, her daughter had fallen into her footsteps.

The Bible is very clear that sin and sin tendencies run in family lines. They remain at work until someone of faith goes before the Lord, repents, and claims the forgiveness and cleansing that is provided by the blood that Jesus Christ shed on the cross. This is our hope as Christians. There is also the law of increase at work, so sin will continue to grow, and it will have a diabolical impact. These and other principles function whether you are a person of faith or not. Had either of my parents or I known Jesus, prayed, sought counsel, or learned how to undo the power of this generational iniquity, life would have been vastly different.

Fornication, which is sexual activity before marriage, and teenage pregnancy were evidently working within our family tree. I naively considered abortion to be a rescue plan from a bad situation. I had no thought or consideration that I was carrying a child. In many ways, it was like a dental problem that needed attention. Nonetheless, I was ashamed, and I just wanted to escape the consequences.

I told no one but my family. I only told them because I was legally forced to do so. The doctor advised me to lie and tell everyone else that I was having an ovarian cyst removed. Extended family, friends, and teachers kindly brought gifts and visited me in the hospital. I felt so guilty, inauthentic and defiled as I chose to share the prescribed lie. My deceit was deepening. My reaping was intensifying. Soon it was over, but some of the joy of living was gone.

Over the next few weeks, it became obvious that my boyfriend did not love me at all. He paid for the procedure, but then he kept his distance. My sister and I were at the victory meeting of a local mayor (She thought it would be good for me to get out), and my boyfriend was there with other high school friends. I said hello to him, and he acknowledged me, but he obviously did not want to engage in conversation. I started to walk away, and for some reason, I turned to look at him. It was just in time to see him mocking me to his friends. He thought that I would not see him. At the time, my heart broke again in a new way. It became obvious to me that he had already left me in every sense of the word.

I'd like to say that I had learned my lesson, but I had not. A new boyfriend from our high school was quick to move into the void and offer romance and love again. He promised that he would love and protect me. I thought, *I am older and wiser now*, but a few months later, a broken condom led to a second pregnancy. I was now sixteen and beginning my last year in high school. I was so unhappy with myself and my foolishness. I wanted to go to university. To escape the consequences of my actions, I booked another abortion with the same doctor. He was quite willing to go ahead with the procedure, on the condition that I start taking birth control pills.

I have virtually no memory of the second early pregnancy uterine-scraping procedure. Our worldly minds are very good at justifying our own hurtful sins. If they cannot do that, I have learned that they will wipe away the conscious memories of devastating life events. The shame, fear, and trauma of my failures and self-accusation were so intense that I buried a few painful days of my life. They were buried but not dead.

To this day, I do not remember the event, with one exception. I shared a room with a woman who was five-to-ten years older than I was. We both had the same procedure. She was in the washroom, and she suddenly cried out to me for help. I went in to see what the problem was. There was blood all over, and she said, "Call a doctor!" She was hemorrhaging. I pulled the cord for immediate assistance. I remember the medical people running in and dismissing me. That is the only thing that I remember of my hospital stay. I remained in the hospital a few days, as that was the protocol of the time.

In the years that followed, I worked to excel at university and graduated with an honor's degree in fine arts and then a master's degree in business administration. I suspect that I was striving to compensate for my failures and actions.

Even nonbelievers have a conscience that will bring conviction. We are made in God's image, and part of us knows what is right and what is wrong.

So in my counseling session for my ministry training, I revisited the trauma of my abortions. The Holy Spirit granted me a heightened awareness of the depth of my sin. I was deeply repentant. I wept and realized that I had murdered two of my own children. I began to understand all the connections of generational family sin, our insidious world culture, and my own complicity, which began with what seemed to be innocent, young love. It had become twisted, sin-soaked, and deadly. I became aware and deeply grateful for the forgiveness that was extended to me through faith in Jesus Christ.

I then had a connecting revelation. The four-month miscarriage (sudden in-utero death of one pregnancy) and then the disabilities that Jack was born with were the logical reaping of my own sin. The Bible is very clear. Unconfessed sins and their consequences are passed on to the next generation, and they also defile many people around us.

In Old Testament times, the scriptures tell us that because of the people groups' sin in Canaan, the land itself *vomited* them out. Thus, the land itself is defiled and abhors the sin that we inflict upon it. No wonder we are having so much trouble today in North American society.

Jesus Christ came to set humankind free from the penalty of sin by taking it all upon Himself at the cross. He also desires to set the rest of creation free from the penalty of our sins. We believers have the privilege of being invited to co-labor in these kingdom-of-God missions. The Bible tells us that all creation is groaning and awaiting the manifestation of the sons of God (see Romans 8:18–25). The scriptures also teach that believers have the authority to bring healing, not only to ourselves personally and our family lineage but also to creation.

I know from my dark times that we are likely to feel isolated and afraid in any crisis, whether it's real or imagined. No matter the reason that we suffer, it is the perfect season to seek, find, and commune with Jesus, who is never shocked at our realities. In His omniscience, He knows all of our thoughts and deeds. Even so, in His love, He extends His mercy and grace, fills us with His presence, cleans us up, and encourages us to start afresh as His new creation. Every unconfessed sin, whether purposely hidden or forgotten, is still contributing to our brokenness.

I have learned to daily confess my sins to God, whether they are large or small, in Jesus's name. He is always ready and willing to forgive and reestablish a wonderful rapport. The devil will attempt to thwart, frustrate, or hinder each of us, but our Heavenly Father has provided everything that we need for life and godliness. I have also learned that when I slide into self-condemnation or any other difficulty, I can simply follow the biblical instruction to confess to another person of faith.

The apostle Paul writes, that it is for freedom that Christ has set us free (see Galatians 5:1). I could have stopped so much personal suffering through my repentance, but I was ignorant and without biblical teaching. For many years, I felt like a fraud, and I was filled with guilt. Today, I know that conviction is a gift from the Holy Spirit, which is given so that we will surrender, repent, and return to our Father's will and purposes. Then we can get back on track with our ordained destinies.

I hope that if you have been in a similar situation, you too will stop, pray, confess the things that you have done, and receive forgiveness from Jesus, who is "faithful and just to forgive you your sin and cleanse you from all unrighteousness" (1 John 1:9). He lifts off the burdens and the inner torment. Righteousness, peace, and joy are available to anyone who is willing to yield to His ways and purposes. He really does love and want us to be made whole. Then He directs us to be part of His solution in our broken world. When we cooperate with Him, we can enjoy life without the weight of the past. A life of hope, expectancy of good things, adventure, and even excitement unfold. As a bonus incentive, I know that every sin I confess and bring to God will assist in removing stumbling blocks from the lives of my children and their future generations. God's appointed prosperity is restored.

Even though my life was sometimes hectic and complicated with appointments, decisions, and the cares of the household in those early days, I was recharged and excited after my Wednesday evenings on the ministry team. I received much more than I gave. We heard some of the best preachers and teachers in the western Christian charismatic world. We saw multitudes of miracles and physical and emotional healings. The testimonies were often incredible. The gifts of the Holy Spirit were evident and frequent. We witnessed His marvellous workings in each meeting.

The mentoring women at our weekly home Bible study decided that it was time for me to co-labor as a leader in one of the women's neighborhood groups. I had learned a lot, and I was excited about discipling new believers, so I jumped at the opportunity with great enthusiasm.

Meanwhile my mother had repeatedly told me with great compassion and concern about a woman whom she was mentoring in her life-insurance business. This woman had previously run her own law practice, but she was now unwell and struggling. She was trying to find less demanding work. The more that I heard about her, the more I became convinced that Jesus was ready to help her. I had our Wednesday home group pray for her.

I kept asking my mother to invite her to our Bible study. Finally, they both came. After the meeting, I followed them outside to the car and asked what she thought of the meeting. She replied that she enjoyed it. I then asked if she would come back and join our weekly gatherings. I received a definite, "No." I was disappointed. I could tell that the door was politely but firmly closed. Sometimes we give up before the Lord does. About three weeks later, the Holy Spirit brought her to my mind. I felt that He was saying, *Call her.* That happened again and again for several weeks over the following six months. I always kept the calls short and prayed for healing.

One day, she abruptly said, "Laurel, why do you keep calling?"

Somewhat taken aback, I replied, "I call when I think the Holy Spirit tells me to, but if I am bothering you, I can stop calling. Am I bothering you?"

She replied, "No, I just wondered." That response emboldened me somewhat. I asked again if she would consider coming to a meeting and added that they were now in my home. Her response was still negative.

Then I surprised both of us. "Can I come to see you?"

A long pause followed this, and then she said, "Yes."

A time was scheduled, and our visit was pleasant. I took her through the Billy Graham ministry booklet, as I often had done at the church with new believers. I then asked her to sign the new contract that she had with her heavenly Father and His Son, Jesus, her Lord and Savior. I think that the covenant-contract signing at the back of the booklet resonated with her legal training, so we then prayed.

Afterward, I was full of a God-given boldness and faith, so I encouraged her by saying, "If you come each week to our Wednesday group and let us lay hands on you each time, I know the Lord will heal you." She looked astounded. My faith was supernatural but real. I was completely convinced. It was the gift of faith in action.

Over the next eighteen months, she did come, and we did lay hands on her. Chronic fatigue and fibromyalgia symptoms disappeared. Her diagnosed dead thyroid was completely regenerated. She gave up her thyroid medication, bought a guitar for twenty dollars at a neighborhood street sale, rediscovered her love of music, wrote inspired Christian songs, and became our worship leader. Elaine is a wonder, and her story could easily be another book.

As weeks and months passed, I continued my daily responsibilities while my internal desire for the Holy Spirit's fire grew and grew. Once a month, the women leading the neighborhood Bible study groups met. At one of these meetings, the Lord allowed me to experience His healing power physically.

One of our more senior saints, our beloved Aunt Harriet, had a very large breast lump that was scheduled to be removed surgically. They had ruled out a biopsy for fear of spreading cancer cells. Toward the end of the meeting as we were concluding our prayer time, she looked at me intently and asked if I would lay my hand on the lump directly and pray. Of course, I would, and I did. As I began to pray, intermittent surges of power pulsated outwardly, seemingly from my elbow, down through my hand, and then on to dear Aunt Harriet. I could tell she felt it too. She jerked as if electrically shocked with each power surge. We were both stunned, silent, and in awe.

It was the end of the meeting, so I quietly and quickly gathered my things and left, feeling very shaky. I cried in the car on the way home. I felt unworthy and elated. I also desperately prayed that this was more than a feeling and that the healing would manifest.

I phoned her later that afternoon and told her how awestruck I was. She told me that the moment she had stepped inside her apartment and closed the door, she had been graced with holy laughter for about twenty minutes. A few days later, she did have the surgery. The laboratory test stated that the lump was not cancer but benign and dealt with. Praise God. Hallelujah!

I have not physically felt that same power surge again. I wondered if this was the Lord encouraging me to keep pursuing healing prayer and to build my faith, or was He answering His beloved Harriet's prayers and faith? We never know the ways and purposes of God completely. He alone knows and directs our journey toward wholeness, which is provided in His presence and goodness. I respect and pray for all healing evangelists who are willing to risk their reputations to pray for healing for others. I had tasted the thrill and joy that they experience as they spread and minister the power of the gospel's good news and co-labor in this much-needed ministry, which draws so many of us into a deep and unshakeable faith in Jesus Christ.

CHAPTER 5

The Trust Test

I learned a lot about the Father-heart of God, but knew there was so much more. To keep the boys busy over the Christmas holidays, after Christmas, Bob enrolled the three older boys in skiing lessons. Eventually, they would be experienced enough to instruct. They stayed up north in a rented place, and I stayed home with Jack. I had tried to go up with Jack, but it had been very difficult because the rental place had been inconvenient in many ways. It was easier for us to stay home, especially for Jack. He hated long drives.

I had already spent a number of years at the Toronto Airport Church (now called Catch the Fire), hearing all the messages and preaching about the loving Father-heart of God. I decided that for New Year's Eve while I was home with Jack, I would read the gospel accounts of the Last Supper. I would then take communion and ask the Lord to give me a revelation of His love and heart for me. I understood it intellectually, and I was aware of His close presence, but I suspected that there was a lot more.

After Jack was in bed, I began reading the biblical accounts of Jesus sitting with His disciples and having the

Passover meal with them—His last one on earth. There He instructed His disciples and proclaimed the new covenant. His body would be broken as the bread of heaven and the word made flesh. He instructed the disciples to remember to eat of Him and ingest all that He was, until His presence and life manifested through them. The wine represented His blood, which was to be shed sacrificially as the Lamb of God for the forgiveness and remission many people's sins.

I read through Matthew, Mark, and Luke, but as I searched in the last gospel, John, I realized for the first time that there was no specific account of the Last Supper that was comparable with the other gospels. Instead, there was the story of Jesus taking off his outer clothes, wrapping a towel around Himself, and like a servant, washing the disciples' feet. I had an aha moment as I realized that the much-loved gospel's author (John) was telling us that humbling ourselves and serving others was, in many ways, just as important as taking communion—the bread and wine—in remembrance of Jesus and His instructions.

I proceeded to give thanks, prayed awhile, and then took the communion elements. It was close to midnight as I sat reflecting in our bedroom. I said aloud, "Father, I want to know You, what this Father-heart-of-God message means to me, and how it applies to my life."

In my imagination, I pictured myself as a little girl of seven or eight in a party dress, which in real life did not happen very often. I could see the secondhand, checkered dress of cream and yellow-gold that I wore at around that age. There was a particular school-children's birthday party that I had attended. My mother had put small yellow roses in my blond hair to match the dress. I felt very elegant and special. With that memory in my mind, I pictured myself sitting on what I can only describe as the Father's holy lap of glory. His form was a fiery, blinding light, which was both awesome and uniquely comforting. I leaned back, snuggling into His presence.

All of a sudden, Holy Spirit took over my self-created mental video. There was a Tootsie Roll Pop in my mouth. To my surprise, I realized that I used to really like them when I was young, and I had often spent the few cents that I had had to buy one. It was as if the Father was saying, *I know all about you, your history, and your desires.* He even knew the candy that I preferred at that age.

Then all of a sudden, He burst forth and expanded explosively, seemingly larger than the size of the universe. I was a tiny speck floating like a little amoeba in the sea of His creation and presence. It actually frightened me. A jolt of adrenaline surged within as my heart pounded. He immediately became the more human size I had first imagined Him to be. He said to me in an inner quiet voice, *I am as big or as small as you need me to be.* His profound and personal kindness in the midst this display of His almighty power was inspiring and very comforting. His love for me was suddenly real and inexplicably trustworthy. I could overcome anything *in Him*. He was almighty as well as my Daddy God.

A few days later, I was invited to join a new women's small group, which was headed up by Mary Audrey Raycroft, the leader of women's ministry in our church. I was both flattered and surprised because I did not think she even knew who I was in such a large and busy congregation. I was excited by this new opportunity. Our little group began to meet, and she invited us to a teaching session in a church near Niagara Falls. Liberty Savard was teaching on the power of prayer and the real effects and impact of binding peoples' minds to the mind of Christ according to scripture (see Matthew 18:18 and 1 Corinthians 2:16) and binding peoples' feet to the path of righteousness. It was followed by an intense time of ministry.

As we were leaving, our leader said to me and my friend, "I believe the Holy Spirit wants me to take you two with me on my upcoming mission trip to Australia." First I was shocked, and then I then scoffed internally.

My doubt and unbelief only increased as we drove the two hours home. When my friend asked me about the possibility of my going on this mission trip, I quipped, "I have never left Jack even for twenty-four hours. I am not going to the other side of the world for two weeks." Her encouragement fell on ears that were deaf to her arguments. I knew she wanted us both to go.

Later without my knowledge, she went back to speak with our leader. She said, "Laurel is not taking this seriously," and she relayed my position and admittedly carnal knee-jerk response. Apparently, they prayed for me. She then came back and said, "Laurel, promise me you will pray and ask the Lord about this."

And I said, "I promise. I will pray." I did not expect that my mind would change.

I do think that the integrity of our words and our commitment to them are important. As believers, we are instructed biblically to let our yes be yes and our no be no. Scripture tells us everything else, including our waffling and doubt, is from the evil one. To be true to my word, I went to my prayer chair in the bedroom and said, *So, Lord, they want me to go to Australia. What do You say?* I sat quietly, expecting nothing.

To my shock, I heard Him whisper, *Do you not trust me with Jack?* In a flash of revelation, I realized He was saying, *Put your Isaac on the altar.* I suddenly had a new appreciation for the struggle that Abraham went through. He must have had to overcome his natural fatherly instincts when he was asked by the Lord to sacrifice his beautiful, much-loved, and promised son.

Isaac was very special to Abraham. He had been miraculously conceived when Abraham was ninety-nine. The almighty God proved Himself to be the master of human frailty and circumstances. Nothing was impossible with Him. Abraham didn't tell anyone what he was going to do, but he obeyed the Lord's request.

His son also trusted and dutifully yielded to his father's intentions. Fortunately for Isaac, an angel stopped Abraham and supernaturally provided a ram with its horns caught in a nearby bush. Abraham gratefully realized that this was the Lord's provision and intervention. Abraham then sacrificed the ram instead of Isaac. God had tested Abraham's faith, love, and obedience, but He had made sure that he passed the test.

I pondered my own modern-day situation. How would my spouse respond to the Lord's request that I go on a mission trip? I certainly couldn't travel to Australia and not tell him. I said, *Okay, Lord, but please help me. I want to trust You. I want to be obedient.* I prayed for the situation and then presented the whole idea and project to my husband. He was skeptical, even as I had been. I tried to explain that I actually did not want to go and agreed it would be difficult. I reasoned with him that if that was his final verdict, I did not have a problem submitting to it. I explained, "It's the leader of our women's ministry, and I think, the Holy Spirit who are asking me to go." We had a quiet evening, and I admit that I was somewhat relieved. I did not have to go.

However the next day, my husband came back with a plan. If I could arrange for our daytime help to move in for two weeks, he would take the three older boys on a car trip to the Maritimes while I was in Australia. So the project was back on, despite my inner conflicting emotions. God had once again made a way.

The day seemed to come too soon. I would take the taxi to the airport and then fly to Australia. I cried on the drive there because I was fearful and unsure that Jack would be all right. Nonetheless, I sensed a supernatural inner strength and conviction that I had to obey, so I willingly yielded to the Lord's plan. This resolve was sufficient to hold me steady through my time away from my family. I was not concerned about having any special role. I was participating because the Lord required it of me. As far as I was able, I would play any part that He had for me. I prayed a lot for Jack's safety, health, and happiness.

Early in our Australian adventure and my inaugural mission trip, I noticed a level of friction between two people in our team. I sensed that a competitive jealousy was brewing. Because of an increasing level of my friend's frustration and her request, I went to the leader. After talking, we agreed that we would get together and pray before each meeting. I thought, *Perfect!* Unity was quickly restored, and the potential problem was solved. In fact, the competitors ended up becoming friends and cooperated with one another even after the trip. Praise the Lord! It could have been an unpleasant cat fight.

The first scheduled meeting was a three-day women's

conference in Canberra, Australia. Our leader was teaching on the spirit of Jezebel, a demonic force that uses manipulation, intimidation, and control. She asked us, as part of the larger ministry team, to walk around the room of about three hundred women and intercede for them. While I was doing that, I noticed that a spirit of slumber came over many of the women in her sessions. The devil did not want people to hear her message.

Have you ever noticed how you can be quite alert until you pick up and begin to read something that is helpful like the Bible? That spirit of slumber works to hinder our spiritual growth and maturity. I have experienced this myself and watched it work on many others. People fall asleep during the most important and impactful part of the message. They are being spiritually blocked from absorbing freeing and important information. When I learned about this, I would sometimes read or pray on my knees to resist this dark interference.

After our first evening meeting in Australia, all of the ministry team met together for a review. The leaders were discussing an attendee who was highly demonized and broken. The leader of their Australian team had spent a lot of time with her, and she was well aware that she had not been successful in setting her free. I knew who they were talking about. We all did.

As I was walking around the room the next morning, I saw this broken woman. She was wandering aimlessly in a large area off to one side, which I was slowly walking through and overseeing. I sent up an SOS flash prayer. *Please, Lord, I think she is too big a ministry project for me, but would you look after her?* I changed my direction a little bit, hoping to avoid any direct confrontation. However, the more I moved, the more she corrected her course and got closer to me. Finally, she fell down on the cement floor at my feet. She was twitching, and her eyes were rolled back in her head. She was obviously in a full-blown demonic manifestation, which was more extreme than anything that I had seen before.

I was aware of other women watching, but I could feel the Lord's compassion for her rising inside me. I quietly said to the Lord, *What now?* while also thinking, *Oh, no!* I got down on my knees beside her and put my hand on her shoulder. I felt great pity, but I was unsure of what to do for her.

The Holy Spirit whispered to me, *Tell her to say "Jesus."* I did that. I could see her trying to speak. I repeated myself. I could see that she was trying to focus her eyes on me and to get her mouth under control.

After what seemed like a long time, she said a garbled, "Jesus."

I said, "Good! Say it again." She said it more clearly. The weird motions were stilled, she composed herself, and then said it again, this time very clearly, with her eyes completely focused, and while looking right at me. Relieved, I said, *Now what, Lord?*

The Holy Spirit said, *Now you can pray in the ways you have been taught to bless her.* I asked the Lord, in his mercy, to touch her, heal her, and bring His restoring power and love to deliver her.

She cried for a while and then sat up. She said, "Can I ask you a question?"

"Yes."

"Is it true that if I smoke a single joint of marijuana, I will be seven times more demonized than I was before?"

I replied, "No. I know the scripture you are referring to. I don't think it is an appropriate reference here. The God I know is very merciful and sees your efforts. You're here at this meeting seeking Him, and He promises that when we seek Him, He will be found by us" (see Matthew 6:33).

She flashed a beaming smile from her thin, worn-out, and very lined face. She then said, "Thank you so much! Hold on just a minute." She leaped up and then started to run around the room like a young horse running free from a tight barn enclosure. I think she did three laps around the huge conference room while everybody else watched and wondered. She was rejoicing all the while. Her exuberant gratitude was powerful. I was obviously in awe.

She finally came back and said, "My minister told me that by smoking joints, I was inviting more demons. I was devastated and almost gave up on God, thinking that I would never be free. Marijuana is nothing compared to what I have already come off." We talked about her forgiving the minister and prayed. I explained that the Word of God actually does say that returning to previous sin does open the door to an increased infection spiritually, but that's why we are exhorted to continually seek and worship the Lord. It keeps us safe in His care.

She then began to tell me some of her history. When she was a young girl, her father and brothers tied her to the bed frame spread-eagled and raped her. When they had finished, her mother came in and beat her. It happened many times. Obviously, as soon as she could, she ran away from home and lived on the streets. She was wooed by a young man whom she believed loved her. In the beginning things seemed fine. However, he facilitated a hard drug addiction and then demanded that she prostitute herself to finance the habit. She fell deeper and deeper into despair. Again, she ran away. She was then in homosexual relationships. Finally, she almost gave up on life itself. She entered into a platonic relationship for mutual safety. She knew she was a wreck.

Finally in her desperation, she began to edge back into the church. She had hoped that in this meeting in Canberra, God would meet her. She was thrilled that He did. She told me that her mother regularly attended church. Oh, the secrets that we keep, the darkness that needs to be discerned, and the deliverance that needs to come within the church. May the Lord help us all.

Then she added, "I want to tell you something else. I saw you coming toward me, and I was praying that I would not manifest demons. I have before, and I did not want to be ashamed in front of you and all these people. And of course, the demons threw me to the ground. I could hear your voice telling me to say, 'Jesus,' and it was a real struggle. When I finally opened my eyes, I want you to know that I did not see you. I saw Jesus. It was so cool. He was here with me, and I thank you for your part."

After lots of hugs and encouragement, I connected her with a Christian woman on the team who lived locally (and who actually knew her mother). The local counselor was very wise and full of grace and mercy. I knew this young woman would be in good hands.

Many wonderful things happened in that meeting. After two days of teaching and ministry, a supernatural joy filled the women so much that a spontaneous water baptism erupted. It began when two of the speakers began to playfully throw water at each other, first from a water bottle and then from a small fountain that had been placed at the front as a decoration. The Holy Spirit joyfully moved on the leaders. The splashing and laughter intensified. They were getting more playful and stood together in the pool, splashing even more. A woman from the audience rushed up and sat down in their midst. Soon every woman lined up to get her turn for a "baptism" in six inches of water. It was ridiculously funny yet glorious. We were all soaked and full of joy. Smiles and laughter broke out everywhere. I will never forget God's goodness toward his daughters, who had come together from many denominations to meet, find healing, and receive more of Him.

From there, our team went to an arranged meeting at an aboriginal reservation in the heart of Australia. The pastor that we went to see visited the community regularly. He told us how they had put in a cement pad that was used as a multipurpose facility with a smooth platform. It was used for basketball games as well as ministry. They had a sound system loaded on a truck. All we would have were floodlights on the pad of cement.

He forewarned us that whenever they went in to minister, stray dogs would come and copulate all around. I was silently outraged and determined that this would not happen on my watch. I began to pray and intercede privately. We arrived in the evening, and the message was given. No dogs copulated at that meeting. I really felt the Father's pleasure that I had used the authority that we all have available through the name of Jesus to cleanse His ministry site.

From there, we traveled and enjoyed a side tourist trip to a canyon river. We traveled on a flat-bottomed boat. Our guide was a very young, well-muscled, and handsome Australian, who explained the rock formations and geographical details. He mentioned that the river was full of crocodiles. We traveled along slowly and enjoyed the beauty of the canyon cliffs and the lush valley's vegetation. We landed at a certain point, and he announced, "I am inviting and will lead anyone who wants to make a one-mile trek inland. I forewarn you, it's a little rugged, with lots of up and down. We will go into the back hills and discover a beautiful double waterfall with a small pool at the bottom. There are no crocodiles that far inland. If you want, you can go swimming. It's worth the walk, if you can manage it, and a very beautiful place to visit."

Our leader decided that she would stay behind, but the rest of us made the trek. It was as outlined—an arduous walk in—but the falls and the scenery were well worth it. We could not see where the waterfall actually came from because the source was high above the soaring, flat cliff's face. Water fell down to a narrow rock ledge, which we could see. Then it fell down again into a pool.

Our guide explained that we could swim a few feet under the pool's water, and with eyes closed, we could aim for the waterfall. With our hands held protectively in front of us, we could swim until we felt the rock's face, stand up, and find ourselves directly under the waterfall. He then demonstrated in his Aussie tour-guide's shorts and shirt.

I am a very good swimmer, so I was pretty determined to try this in my summer top and shorts. First, with all the strength and speed that I could muster, I swam toward the waterfall, doing a front crawl on the surface of the water. There was no way that I could get within five feet of the actual waterfall. There was too much force in the outward push of the current.

The guide smiled at my attempt and repeated, "You

have to go deeper and underneath the surface." So I dove down a couple of feet, following his instructions this time. With my eyes shut tightly against the churning water and hands groping in front of me, I found the rock wall, turned to stand, and sure enough, I came up under the waterfall. It was a revelatory exercise in listening to instructions, obeying them, and trusting. The water's power was so strong that I could only stay under it for a few seconds before it pushed me out. It was both exhilarating and scary.

I really did not want to do it again, but I felt the Lord was saying, *This is a little like being under My glory.* Wet but content, our small troop marched back up the hill, down the dale, through the woods, and back to our boat.

To finish our trip, we went up to Darwin, Australia, where we had a series of successful meetings with Pentecostal churches. One minister, who had come out of a wild motorcycle-biker past, and his wife were particularly anointed to minister to the poor. Every Tuesday, they would take an old secondhand school bus to the downtown area and collect anybody who wanted to come to their church service. On arrival, they were part of a fifteen-minute worship time and a quick message. Then everyone had lunch together.

The minister told me that they always made either soup or stew with vegetables to provide good nutrition and that they had seen sores on children's legs healed after only a couple of weeks on this once-a-week nutritious meal. I was impressed. He added, "I always eat with them. It has to taste good enough for me for it to be good enough for them." I loved the humility of this team of God's servants, the practical work being done, and their spiritual hearts to give and help the downtrodden and poor.

As the grand finale, the pastors took us to a crocodile

farm, which ultimately explained to me the reason that they had not taken us to the waterfront or beach. There were big crocs in those waters. As we entered the gates of the farm, I could feel the anointing of the Holy Spirit increasing, which I now knew was a cue and an alert for me to pay attention.

As we entered the grounds, we saw a pond of dark water. Our guide asked us how many crocodiles that we thought were in there. We could see about ten or twelve sunning themselves or poking their noses out. We started to make guesses. He informed us that there were over seventy. We were shocked. They were well hidden. He told us that they stayed in formation and waited. If a little dog or other animal came to lap at the waters' edge, the lead crocodile would go after the animal first. If any of the other crocodiles got out of line, the stronger crocodile would chomp off its limb to reestablish its position. Those jaws could come down with between one and two tons of pressure. There was no escape. It would twist and turn its victim until it drowned or bled to death.

They then took us in to see holding pens that were about the size of a squash court. These small cement pens were below our viewing area, and they held about three or four feet of water at a sloped end. That was the deepest part. It gave us a great view of these powerful reptiles. They then hung a chicken on a wire eight feet up. Did you know that crocodiles can jump? They can propel themselves out of the water and grab a hanging chicken in a flash, with a twisting movement that shoots them upward.

We were informed that they could also run up to thirty kilometers (nineteen miles) an hour for a short distance. It was truly gruesome, but it got worse.

We went into the museum and saw photos of the damage these reptiles had inflicted. Boats were bitten, people lost body parts, and in one horrible case, a young boy was swallowed whole. They caught, killed, and split the crocodile open, but the boy had already perished. There he lay, looking perfect but lifeless. These reptiles were ten to fourteen feet long and ferocious.

The anointing of the Holy Spirit within me was getting really potent. We walked through a shop where you could buy boots, hats, belts, and all kinds of things made with crocodile skin. At the very end of the tour, we were invited to hold a baby crocodile, which was about a foot and half long. Its snout was closed shut with an elastic band. Tourists had pictures taken of them holding the crocodiles.

I heard the Holy Spirit say, *Do not touch one of those.* My friends all had their pictures taken, and they were pressing me to have a picture taken. In obedience to the Holy Spirit, I quietly refused (I did not really want to anyway). Then the Lord whispered inside of me, *Do not ever toy with the demonic, even a small demon. It is not a game. Do not touch them unless I tell you to.*

Yikes and yes, Sir! I thought inwardly. Thank You, Lord, that you warn us and keep us safe.

We returned to Sydney, and we had another boat tour around the beautiful city and harbor. After a walk and a last look, we flew home. Praise the Lord that Jack and the family were fine. I realized that I had been in a divinely ordained and very personal school of the Holy Spirit. It was awesome. I had been so reluctant to go to Australia, but now, my heart was changed. I was now praying that He would arrange another mission trip for me in the future.

CHAPTER 6

Pastor's Lunch and Hospital Rescue

One day in our little church, Conor asked if I could go to his Christian school for a pastors' luncheon, as his guest and pastor. I was quite touched. It was my first official function as an ordained pastor outside of our home church. It was a lovely event. I was the only woman pastor in the room. As the high school worship students were leading us in worship, I could feel the Lord's pleasure. I quietly and under my breath I said, "You really like this place, don't you, Lord?"

He quickly and clearly responded, *I really love this place.* I was surprised to hear His voice with such emphasis, so a few days later while back at our women's group, I told them about the situation. I asked if they would be willing to take up an offering and fund some kind of a scholarship program. I thought that maybe the other pastors would like to contribute. We ended up raising about $800. I decided to call it the Shepherd's Award and give it to students who displayed Christlike characters.

Elaine and I went to the principal of this private Christian school, who was delighted with our idea and, not surprisingly, was willing to receive the money. I asked at the end of our brief meeting if he would like us to pray for him. Looking surprised, he said, "Oh, yes." Elaine and I went behind him, placed a hand on his shoulder, and began to pray. Tears ran down his face. Afterward, this burly and authoritative man looked at me through reddened, wet eyes and said, "Would you consider joining our board of directors?"

I smiled compassionately and said, "I don't think so, but thank you for considering me," and then we left.

In the next few weeks, three different people who had children at the school asked me if I would consider joining the board. My answer was always the same, but I began to wonder and asked the Lord in prayer if this was His will and doing. I got a very clear witness that, *Yes, I am asking you to do this.* Subsequently and without any obstacles, I was voted in at their annual, general meeting and one of only two non-parents on the board.

During my first board meeting, I began to understand the principal's distress. The discord and strife levels were shocking. Factions had developed, and angry accusations were flying. Shortly thereafter, the chair of the board resigned, and a new one was elected. I was praying that relationships and the business at hand would continue in an orderly fashion, but the discord continued.

Elaine, Conor, and I (and Jack for one day) decided to undertake an upcoming holiday March Break Bible Camp at the school. For five days, we held a program for about a dozen young children.

We started each day with worship, prayer, and a Bible story time. Conor's dad, Owen, came each day to take the campers out on the soccer field and teach them some skills. Then they would play a soccer game. We made crafts, and usually at that time, we would ask if anyone wanted prayer for anything. The day ended with a joyful cha-cha dance that my sister used with her grade three class.

My brother-in-law, a Royal Canadian Mounted Police officer, and his family also came to make presentations about the police force in Canada and its history. They also introduced new games and added to the fun.

Wonderful things happened in those five days. One young girl who was known for being very rebellious stirred up trouble each day. I took her aside and said, "You are a born leader. You need to decide whether you are going to lead people into trouble or into something that is good. I see that you like the cha-cha dance. Why don't you get up and be the leader every day?" She was delighted, and that was the beginning of quite a turnaround for her.

There was also a little Muslim boy who came in with a full-time caregiver. He was around five years old. He was a nonverbal, autistic, and busy little guy. On the last day of the week, we were coloring pictures together. We asked each one of the group for prayer requests. Then we all prayed together for that child.

We were almost finished when I realized that the little boy had not had prayer. So I pulled up a little chair, sat in front of him, and told him it was his turn to get prayer. I looked at him and began to pray a simple blessing. The Holy Spirit was amazing! The child actually engaged with me, gazing deeply into my eyes. We were told this very unusual. Then he became very still, which again was unusual for him, put his hand up, and caressed my cheek.

His full-time caregiver started to cry and told me

that she had never seen him do that. At that point, she expressed her desire to become a Christian too. That was a very satisfying end to our school Bible camp. Afterward, the board meetings seemed to be less toxic and more productive. The atmosphere was slowly shifting.

A little while later, one of my spiritual mothers, who had been recently widowed, yielded to some pressure to get a flu vaccine. She did not really want to because she had a strong faith in Jesus Christ as her healer. Trying to appease well-meaning advisors, she went ahead and got the vaccine. A few weeks later, she told me that perhaps, it had been a mistake. She felt that her immune system became weak and that an ear infection could be traced to the injection. Unfortunately, her ear infection got worse. The next thing that I heard was that she had developed meningitis and that she was unconscious in the hospital across the street from our home. I was horrified.

I asked one of her daughters if Elaine and I could visit together and pray for her mother. What disturbed me the most was our conversation, and I paraphrase what she said: "She is eighty-six and has had a good life," suggesting it was okay if she died. I am not opposed to anyone going home to heaven, and I knew she would, but she did not have to go in a way that brought no glory to her Lord. I did not feel that it was the Lord's will or time.

With that conviction in mind, Elaine and I got permission to visit her in the hospital. I had a two-hour window on a Saturday morning when someone was coming to look after Jack. The rest of the family was up north skiing. As Elaine and I prayed and walked over to the hospital, we began to chuckle. We felt like we were in the movie Ghostbusters, as we went in to get rid of the demons that were afflicting and hanging around our beloved sister in Christ.

On arrival at the hospital, it became obvious that we had arrived an hour before official visiting hours started, but as time was of the essence due to my babysitting arrangements, we went in anyway. As unobtrusively as we could be, we searched and found our friend with her daughter. We prayed for and laid hands on our unconscious friend. Then we prayed for her daughter. After less than half an hour, we left, feeling very confident that the Lord had heard our prayers.

Praise God for His faithfulness. Our dear friend did come out of the coma. Shortly thereafter, we went back with communion elements. I am happy to report that she made a speedy and complete recovery. Our friend went on to enjoy many Christian exploits in the following years, which would have been lost if she had gone to heaven too early. She had the privilege of seeing one of her grandsons enter the ministry successfully, grow his church, and give her a place of honor as a church intercessor.

Week by week and over many years, women continued to meet for worship, Bible study, and prayer, every Wednesday afternoon in our home. We got to know each other very well. At the end of every meeting, people would take turns sitting in what we called the prayer chair and receive the laying on of hands, words of knowledge, words of wisdom, or prophecy. We would allow all the gifts of the Holy Spirit to flow freely.

One particular day, a friend was sitting in the chair and experiencing a deep brokenness about not having children. At that moment, Jack was eating in the kitchen with our caregiver, and he let out a big wail. I quickly went to see if there was a problem, but there did not seem to be anything wrong. Perplexed, I rejoined the group that was praying. Again he cried out. This time when I went to the kitchen, I was inspired to ask him, "Did you want to pray too?"

He gave me a big kiss, *Yes*. I carried him into the living room and explained what had happened. Our friend gladly received him on her lap so that he could intercede for her as she wept. It was a gloriously anointed moment. The Lord's presence and anointing increased noticeably. That was the first time that we had Jack join our prayer sessions. Our heavenly Father truly uses the weak and foolish to confound the wise and strong. We were all baffled and delighted.

A few years later, a pastor from the northeastern area of the United States visited our Wednesday women's group. In the middle of our meeting, Jack came home from school, and as per usual, the women greeted Jack as his wheelchair was rolled into the house. I don't remember the reason why, but I felt a nudge to ask, "Jack, would you like to pray for the pastor?"

He indicated a big, *Yes*, with a kiss, so we brought his wheelchair into the living room.

The pastor looked surprised for a moment but came over, knelt beside the wheelchair, and humbly said, "Lord, say what You want to say to me through this child."

I laid Jack's hand on the pastor's arm, and Jack vocalized his prayer, ending it with a kiss for his, *Amen*. Jack was then taken to the kitchen to have a snack. The fact that Jack waited to have his snack to say this prayer confirmed in my mind that the Holy Spirit was definitely at work.

The next day, we had a smaller meeting with only a few of us. The pastor asked for prayer because while he had received the gift of a large church building, he could not seem to grow his congregation. We spoke and prayed about a number of things. He then told me that he had an adult daughter whose condition was much like Jack's. I asked if the daughter lived with them and his answer was, "No, she is in a home."

I looked at him, hesitated, but then boldly and kindly as I could, said, "Why would God give you more children if you don't look after the ones you have?" I could see he was thunderstruck. We prayed a little bit longer about the congregation, the building itself, his maturing and taking his place in a renewed way as a father of the faith, who was free to reproduce as well as disciple and care for his sheep. We prayed God would bless him to skillfully shepherd his extended family and to add to their numbers.

CHAPTER 7

Master of Ceremonies, End-Time Handmaidens and Servants

Our church was having a women's conference, and for the first time, I was asked to be the master of ceremonies for one of the sessions. While part of me was excited, another part of me was very nervous. This invitation triggered all of my insecurities. To cope, I wrote a word-for-word script of what I was going to say. My script included any scriptures that I would refer to and announcement details that I knew would be important to set up the session.

Just before the meeting began, Mary Audrey Raycroft, our leader, came and told me that among the hundreds attending, there was a small group of women from Winnipeg who called themselves the End-Time Handmaidens and Servants. In the meeting on the previous night, each woman in this group had received a healing miracle. Apparently before being healed, one of the women had experienced such extreme pain that she had been prepared to go to a hospital emergency room with heart-attack symptoms.

I was instructed by our leader. "Laurel, call them up and let them give their testimonies in your introduction."

My first reactions were fear and anxiety about having to go off script. I also knew that I would be expected to pray for them on stage. I had prayed for hundreds of people but never done it publicly on a stage. In obedience, I called them up, hoping and praying that the Holy Spirit would help me. A group of seven or eight women came up. They shared their experiences of healing from the previous night and gave marvelous testimonies. Their excitement was contagious.

I quickly decided that it would be simplest if I selected only one woman to pray for. I would then send the rest of the women down to the ministry team on the floor below the podium, thus limiting the public input that was required of me. I selected the closest woman to me. She was truly excited by the Lord's healing gift, grace, and power. I appreciated her joy and put my hand on her shoulder to pray, when out of my mouth fell these words, "And upon this rock I will build my church, and the gates of hell will not prevail against it" (Matthew 16:18). I was stunned. Those words had not passed through my mind. The Holy Spirit had poured them out of my mouth spontaneously.

Then I felt condemned because I knew the New Testament says a prophet has control over his own spirit. I wondered, *What just happened? What rock was He talking about? The rock of Jesus? The revelation of Him as Messiah? Healing prayer? The End-Time Handmaidens and Servants, whoever they were?* In fact, I thought that the name End-Time Handmaidens was very peculiar. Fortunately, my part was finished. I did not speak about my inner turmoil to anyone. I kept wondering, and off and on over the coming week, I asked the Lord about it. It was a very humbling experience.

Several months later, the leader of our women's ministry

came to our small group with a list of all the places where she would be speaking in the coming year. Many of them were wonderful places to visit, even without the added draw of ministry as an incentive. On the list, there was an End-Time Handmaidens and Servants meeting sponsored by the Winnipeg Branch at a retreat north of Winnipeg. I quickly piped up and said, "I want to go to Winnipeg."

One of the others looked quizzically at me. "Why on earth are you so keen to go to Winnipeg?" I wish I had the inner strength to explain, but I really did not know what the Lord was leading me to or why. I was curious. I wanted to find out the reason that those words had seemingly fallen out of my mouth at the women's conference. It was agreed, and I went along with three others as my leader's ministry team for the small conference at this retreat center.

At the retreat, I found myself sitting back and watching the people in attendance. It seemed to me that they had everything spiritually that we had in the Toronto church in terms of the presence of the Lord, good messages, and manifestations of the Holy Spirit, but there was something else that was there. I wondered if it was because a lot of the people were from a Mennonite background. There were also quite a few First Nations' attendees, as well as Winnipeg city dwellers.

That night I had a dream. Our leader was speaking at the front. I was at the back of the room. A young woman came and asked Jesus to help her. She opened up her blouse, and I could see that she had been whipped on the front of her torso. The scars were restricting the development of her young breasts. Everything was puckered and marred. It was really horrifying. I saw Jesus come out of me and kneel down in front of her with deep compassion. He gently touched her scars and brought immediate healing. I could see how pleased He was that she had trusted Him enough to show Him what had happened to her.

I realized a lot of this was symbolic, and I shared the dream with our leaders, who requested that I share the dream at the morning session. That sparked their scriptural reflections and an intense time of ministry. The Holy Spirit was present to bring healing for anyone who would bring their scars, wounds, and pain to Him.

Toward the end of our conference, it was announced that they were now ready to invite people who had fasted and prayed, and thus, were prepared to come forward to say their vows and consecrate themselves to the Lord as part of the End-Time Handmaidens and Servants' ministry. All of the women and men were dressed in white, except for our little visiting team.

I had never seen anything like it. They recited a prayer of consecration together. Four individuals then said their vows and a blessing was pronounced over them. The others gathered around each of the four novices in little holy clusters and prophesied and prayed over them. I could feel the pleasure and presence of the Lord. I felt like I was privileged to be a witness in some kind of modern-day convent or monastery. Prayers went on for a long while.

When it was time to drive back to Winnipeg and the airport, there was not enough room for all of us on the visiting team to be in the Winnipeg branch leader's car. I was assigned to drive back with one of the women who had just said her vows. With only two of us in the car on the two-hour trip back to Winnipeg, I asked my many questions about the ministry, the vows, the white clothes, and so on. She explained to me that everyone in the ministry had completed a twenty-one-day fast.

I was shocked. I had never fasted for more than one day. I asked her how she had found the fast, and I told her that I was nervous about doing such a prolonged fast because I carried our disabled son up and down stairs in our home. I was afraid I might pass out if I didn't eat.

I remember her laughing and saying, "Oh, no! The first three days are difficult, and you have to be committed and disciplined. But then you'll feel stronger than you have ever felt before. It is actually a wonderful time." Everything that she said was resonating within my spirit, and I wanted to do this fast.

The next few months were busy with family affairs and pre-Christmas preparations. After the holidays, I finally sat down, prayed, and counted out twenty-one days. The desire to fast had only grown within me. The final day of the fast would be February 14, and I felt the Holy Spirit was saying, *Do it as a love letter to Jesus.* That confirmed it, and I began the fast. My friend in Winnipeg was correct. After three days, it felt like the sails had been raised on my little sailboat. I was energized and feeling strong spiritually and naturally. I had no problem making food for the family or doing other day-to-day chores that I was called to do. I felt full, satisfied, and alive. I was aware that there was a great supernatural grace helping me. I will concede that the fasts I have done since then have not been quite so easy.

The twenty-one-day fast became an accelerator and a doorway to a new level of spirituality, confidence, and authority. Most of my friends and family expressed concerns for what they thought was an extreme sacrifice, but I was sure that the Holy Spirit was preparing me for a new dimension of holiness. I realized that it was holiness that I had seen in most of the members of the End-Time Handmaidens and Servants ministry. The founder, Sister Gwen Shaw, had been obedient and anointed to raise up disciples, intercessors, and missionaries, under the direction of the Lord. Holiness seemed to be a byproduct.

The following year in 2008, I heard that Sister Gwen was going to be a conference keynote speaker in Jerusalem within the ministry of Sadhu Sundar Selvaraj. I knew that Sister Gwen respected his prophetic ministry. There were also several other well-known speakers. I was determined to go. I wanted to meet Sister Gwen and have her lay hands on me for the impartation of the ministry, as well as see the Holy Land.

Unfortunately when I arrived in Israel, I found out that she was not well and that she would not be attending. That was a huge disappointment. However, there was still so much to be excited about. After all, I was in Israel in a conference tent that was set up on the Mount of Olives for Sadhu's first Israeli convention. It overlooked the Kidron Valley, the spectacular Jerusalem city skyline, its ancient walls, and the bricked up Gate Beautiful, along with the controversial Dome of the Rock.

The tour that followed the convention was interesting intellectually and stimulating spiritually. An outstanding moment for me took place on a hot afternoon that we spent on Mount Carmel. We walked over lightly trodden paths and rocky terrain until we came to a clearing, which was high up on the mountain, overlooking the beautiful farmland and the Jordan River. Cows meandered lazily through the trees, munching as they went with their bells ringing quietly. Late spring wildflowers and grasses decorated the hills.

When we gathered, Sadhu preached on the prophet Elijah and his confrontation with the false prophets of Queen Jezebel. He biblically explained what had happened in the area that we were in and preached about the significance for our day. Then he asked each of us to make a little altar with any chosen number of stones that we could find. We were instructed to prayerfully inquire of the Lord the sacrifice that He wanted us to put on the altar. The group spread out, and we diligently built and prayed.

I selected three hand-sized stones from the loose ones around me and asked the Lord, *What or who do I need to put on my altar of sacrifice? What do You want me to give to You?*

I thought He was going to say, *Give me Jack*, because Jack consumed so much of my life, prayer time, and energy. To my surprise, the Lord said, *Give me Michael*. Michael is our eldest son. I was shocked, and in a flash of revelation, I realized that Michael had become my place of comfort. He had only been nine when Jack was born, but he had observed our many distresses. He was sweet, compassionate, and always eager to help. I realized that the Lord wanted me to find my comfort and strength in and through Him alone. I repented of making our children idols and substitute comfort in the place of the Lord. By faith and in prayer, I laid Michael on my altar, put him in God's hands, and blessed him.

People often say, "God is always on time." Releasing my emotional hold on our son was a good thing because less than a year later, he met a delightful young woman while working at a Christian summer camp, and they subsequently married. I believe my prayer had set him loose from my incorrect relational bond so that he was free to join more fully with his new love and wife.

In 2011, I went back to Israel. This time, I specifically went with the End-Time Handmaiden's ministry. I was praying that Sister Gwen would be well and strong enough to be there this time. I talked one of my sisters into coming with me, and we had a wonderful excursion. I enjoyed getting to know the core ministry's people and visiting the ministry's House of Peace in Jerusalem. Sister Gwen held a convention in Jerusalem in the middle of our tour. It was attended by about 150 people, and it brought us together with several important and impactful local people, churches, and ministries.

As a special side trip, my sister arranged for us to visit a Jewish childhood friend who had traveled to visit Israel after high school. She had worked on a kibbutz, and subsequently, she had decided to make Aliyah, making Israel her permanent home. There she met and married her husband, and now, she had four adult children. The kibbutz was close to Jerusalem, so we arranged to be picked up at our hotel. We shared Shabbat dinner in her home and met all her children.

We toured the kibbutz and talked about its history and fallen heroes. In the early years, the kibbutz was a farm, but since then, it had been sold to a winery, and the entire commune and business model had shifted. When her children were little, all the children lived in a communal nursery, only visiting their parents on Shabbat. Parents had to work hard on the kibbutz. Over the years, the socialist childcare model had shifted until the nursery resembled a North American day care center, with children living with their parents outside working hours. On our tour,

our friend showed us their community bomb shelter. Her youngest adult son and his friends had turned it into their band's music studio. They had egg cartons on all the walls for the sound, and they were having fun like any young rock bank. We stayed and listened to a couple of their songs and then continued on our tour.

Some months later at home, I had a dream. In this night vision, I noticed that Jack was missing from the house. I went looking in the neighborhood for him. As only dreams can be, it seemed logical that he had managed to take himself to some desired destination. I went into a room that looked like the music studio that the young men in Israel had converted from the bomb shelter. In this dream, a young band of seven men were jamming and enjoying making music together in the studio. Jack was actively engaged in this, and they were joyfully cranking up the music volume. Although it was loud, the music was very spiritual, and I began to joyfully spin and dance in the Spirit. When they finished, the leader of the band looked at me and said, "I bet you would like a CD of that, wouldn't you?"

I eagerly replied, "Yes please." He gave me a sweet smile and shook his head that it was not going to be possible. The next moment, I saw these same young men skiing *up* a mountain. I could see their tracks in the snow. They were having so much fun. They all swooshed to a stop when they got to the top. It seemed as if I were standing right in front of them. Astonishingly as I looked, each one had a huge flame over his head. I thought of Moses turning to see the burning bush. I also thought of the disciples receiving the power and presence of the Holy Spirit after waiting on the Lord in the upper room at Pentecost.

I somehow knew intuitively that all of the young men had been disabled in their lifetimes but that they were now healed—Jack included. Now they were perfect, radiant, joyful, and anointed with the fire of God and the Holy Spirit. They looked like a living menorah (the seven-branched gold lampstand that stood in Moses's tabernacle in the wilderness). When I woke up and reflected, the dream served to fuel my hope for supernatural healing in Jack's future.

To my great delight in 2005, a Toronto branch of the End-Time Handmaidens and Servants were having meetings in our Airport Church. Paul Keith Davis and Bobby Connor were coming to minister alongside Sister Gwen Shaw and the Canadian leadership team of the ministry.

In one of the sessions, my friend and I were sitting in the middle of a row, in the middle section of the large sanctuary. It was at the end of one of Paul Keith Davis's morning messages. He stopped suddenly, looked at me, and said, "You, come up here. There is a lot of light around you. And bring your friend beside you."

I was quite stunned and wondered, *Me?* In my surprise, I remember thinking, *How does this happen?* We were surrounded by people. Intrigued and excited, my friend and I went forward, and the minister and his wife prayed and laid hands on us. We both felt like we had been hit by a lightning bolt, were slain in the Spirit, and lay flat on our backs, shaking violently from head to toe for close to an hour. It felt glorious and strange. I had no idea what it was about, but I enjoyed it all. Our God's glory and power is exhilarating.

My friend that had gone forward with me was very

involved in Christian film production, and she had a chance to speak with Paul Keith Davis on the following day. He wanted to know what she did so that he could pray for her. Then he asked about me. My friend sheepishly told me later that she told him, "She's not in ministry, is married, and has four sons, one of whom is very disabled." She told me that he looked perplexed. I was perplexed too but was grateful for the experience of God's touch.

A few years later with two girlfriends from our Wednesday women's group, I tried to start our own Toronto branch of the End-Time Handmaidens and Servants, at a time of day that I could manage. The previous branch had been disbanded. We had an extremely difficult time opening up this new extension. We could not seem to find the opening, timing, or leading of the Lord.

Then one day, I received a phone call asking if we could gather together some other End-Time Handmaidens and Servants in the area and host a meeting with Sister Gwen. She was traveling and visiting family in the area. Here was our door of opportunity. In November of 2008, Sister Gwen came to our first branch meeting in our church and spoke to around 120 women and a few men. Her reputation was quite a draw.

The following month when Sister Gwen was no longer with us, the numbers fell to about forty or fifty people. Several people in attendance were disappointed that Sister Gwen was not coming, as they had expected to hear her every month. I explained that she was a world-traveling missionary with a base in Arkansas, USA. Toronto was far from her home. We would continue without her while remaining under her mantle and ministry.

For our third meeting, a First Nations' Christian, Kenny

Blacksmith, was free to come. He gave his testimony to about twenty of us. He told us the reason that he had become an End-Time Servant. He had been in Israel at a Feast of Tabernacles' celebration. During the message at the feast, the question was posed as to where each person found his or her identity. Was it in ministry, title, or position? He had felt led of the Lord to take his First Nations' chief headdress and moccasins up to the front and lay them down on the stage altar before God. They symbolically represented his identity, and he surrendered it all to the Lord.

Sister Gwen had been in that same meeting watching. She heard the Holy Spirit say, *Behold your son.* She was intrigued, but she made no effort to approach him.

He had later approached her and said, "While you were preaching, I heard the Holy Spirit say to me, *Behold your mother.*

Their relationship had deepened. Kenny completed the twenty-one-day fast that all ministry members undertake, and through the laying on of hands by Sister Gwen, he received a mantle for intercession and impact in Jesus's name in the nations.

In our Toronto meeting, Kenny encouraged the few of us who were there to strongly consider entering our own twenty-one-day fast. Several in the room were moved by the Holy Spirit, and they agreed to begin. My greatest encouragement came from two women from our Wednesday group, who were both over seventy-five years old. It's exciting to see that the Lord never thinks that we are too old to take on new challenges and begin new chapters in our walk with Him. Moses began his true ministry at eighty. He lived fruitfully and with God's blessings until he was 120. Let us expectantly contend for the same.

Our little branch of End-Time Handmaidens and Servants began to grow. In the spring of 2010, Mike Bickle, from the International House of Prayer in Kansas City, came to speak at Airport Church. In a regular evening church service, he released a prophetic word that declared the beginning of a new decade and move of God. I felt like the Holy Spirit said, *You can now host an End-Time Handmaidens and Servants' convention here.* I began to pray.

A couple of months later, I flew down to the ministry's American convention in July. Over lunch, I told Sister Gwen what I thought I had heard. She smiled, obviously delighted, and announced to everyone at the hospitality lunchtime table, "Let's do it!" I told her that I only had one request: Along with her, Sharon and Philip Buss would come and lead worship. I believed that they carried the heart and worship sound of the ministry. All was agreed upon.

In August of 2010, we hosted our conference. Kenny Blacksmith spoke, as well as Sister Gwen, Dean Bye from Return Ministries, and Frank Seamster. As we were preparing to begin, the Holy Spirit showed me a vision telling me, *I want Jack and your church group to lead worship one morning during the convention.* That surprised me.

So Elaine, Conor, Jack, and I opened the morning of the second day's meeting with worship. My husband had to work very hard to get Jack to the church on time. With Jack draped over my lap, we began worship. The moment we began to sing the songs from our home church, Jack began to beam. The joy on his face was absolutely contagious.

The paparazzi instinct within the congregation emerged, and their cameras took pictures and videos. Truly, the Holy Spirit had ignited something. Even a disabled child could release the power of the joy of the Lord.

CHAPTER 8

Mission Trips and Italy

When Jack was very little, I asked a massage therapist that I had used and liked if she would come to the house and give Jack massages in the hope that she could bring comfort to his body, which was always so tense. She agreed, and for about a year, she would come once a week. I remember that at the end of one session, she looked very sad, and I asked her what the problem was. While at the door before she left, she shared her burden.

She was wondering if she and her husband had made a mistake immigrating to Canada from Poland. They had been trying to conceive a baby. Nothing had happened over many months, and her husband seemed very unhappy. She thought that perhaps, she was depressed.

Because I was fresh from the Holy Spirit meetings in Airport Church, I confidently explained that according to the world-traveling and healing evangelist Bill Subritzky, both anti-Semitism in the family and family involvement in secret societies of any kind were the root causes of 80 percent of all health issues. I asked her if she wanted to pray with me to forgive and remove the effects of her former ancestors (her parents) and other national thoughts, words, and deeds that reflected anti-Semitic attitudes and tendencies. She could then receive forgiveness for that, as well as forgiveness for involvement in secret societies.

She readily agreed, understanding that Poland had been very involved in World War II, Nazism, and the Holocaust, and conceded that residual attitudes were probably very much alive in that nation. So we prayed. I am happy to report that today, she has one child in university and another finishing high school, a prospering husband, and a better life. I believe that prayer opened the door to her restored blessing.

A few years later, I was invited to go with an Italian girlfriend to Italy. I had never been there, so I insisted that we begin with a tour of the Vatican in Rome. At the end of our time in the beautiful Sistine Chapel, we went outside the city wall into a little restaurant to have a much-needed meal. The place was very crowded, and the tiny cloth-covered tables were about two inches apart. Two men were sitting beside us, who were about my age and deep in conversation.

The Holy Spirit said, *Ask them if they are brothers.* I had to ask my friend to ask them in Italian because I did not and still do not speak that language.

They looked surprised and then laughed heartily. "We're priests visiting from Poland." At which point, I laughed too.

Then the Holy Spirit said, *Tell them about your massage therapist and ministry training.* I related the story about the need to repent for anti-Semitism and involvement in secret societies, personally and in our family lines. All of this was being translated back and forth through my friend. I then relayed to them the story of my Polish massage therapist.

When I finished, one of them asked through reverse translation, "What does this have to do with us?"

I answered, "Genesis 12:3 says, 'God said to Abraham, the founding father patriarch of Israel, "I will bless those who bless you, and I will curse him who curses you." I could see that one of the priests got an instant revelation of the way that antisemitism at any level opens the door to curses. The other priest looked very angry.

The Holy Spirit said to me, *Stop talking and eat your meal.* My friend was happy to be relieved of her duty, and the two priests left a few moments later. I said to my friend, "One congregation will get the revelation, and we know which one it is. Lord, may the one inspired priest pray and then exhort the other."

If you have never repented for your own or your ancestors' anti-Semitism, evil thoughts or intents toward Israel, I highly recommend that you take a moment to repent and break the power of and remove curses from your life. Our heavenly Father is faithful to forgive us when we confess and repent in Jesus's name. Our loving Father wants us blessed, but sometimes, specific acts of obedience are required.

Years before I went to Italy, I had a dream that was particularly intense. I think it has partly unfolded to date, but I don't think it has come to completion. In my dream, it felt like I was in Italy, although I had never been there at that point. People were being offered school bus rides to safe areas. Somehow, I knew it was a trap. I was not sure what would happen to them. It was as if they were going to concentration camps, maybe even to be exterminated. I was understandably alarmed.

I began walking down the little streets, which reminded

me of pictures of Italy. I went into a small, dark, cheap, and smoky bar. There at the back in the dingy light, I saw Mel Gibson slouched over a small table, and he was drunk. I went up to him and said, "The people need your help."

He gave me a bleary look, as if to say, "Don't be ridiculous. What am I supposed to do?" At that point, a young woman who was the bartender or waitress came over and started encouraging him with me. Somehow we got him to another safe house, where there were other helpers, and we began making him a costume. On the top of his head where a crown would sit, he wore a replica of the Temple in Jerusalem. From there down and hiding his face, there was a long deep-blue priestly robe. No one could see who he was. He was now sober and willing, and he walked outside of his dressing room and started walking through the street. The people began following him.

I am not exactly sure how the dream ended. I knew that he was leading the people to safety and the care of the Lord. Mel Gibson was willingly searching for more wisdom from the Lord, and he had completely yielded his life in humility so that he could lead others to righteousness and life. He was a very important instrument in the hand of the Lord.

Because of the dream, when my girlfriend asked me to join her prayer walk in Italy, I jumped at the chance. One place that we visited was Matera, Italy. I was surprised to learn on our visit that this town was the place where Mel Gibson had filmed his movie *The Passion of the Christ*. That movie came out quite a while after my dream. Matera had all kinds of tourist spots with pictures of him and his cast filming the movie. It had become a welcome source of tourist income and notoriety for Matera.

The town was very beautiful and an untouched gem of older historic days. The city was set in the fold of ancient hills. Caves in the cliffs of a nearby ravine were occupied over the centuries by holy men and women who desired to be closer to God. Today, shepherds still meander with their flocks along the ravine at the cliff's base. Many years later, Matera and my dream's connection continued, but I have to add another story thread for it to make sense.

My youngest sister's husband walked out of their marriage in an abrupt manner. She was devastated, and she essentially stopped eating in her distress. I arranged for her to go to our Toronto church to receive ministry through Family Foundations, an interactive group ministry founded by Craig Hill. In years past, I had become a trained facilitator for that ministry and ministered in a number of the Family Foundation groups in the church, so I knew what it was all about. Thursday night, Friday night, and all day Saturday, there were video teachings followed by group and small-group ministry. By a prearranged agreement, I was in my sister's group as an intercessor and an added counselor, as needed. That meant, of course, that Jack was at home with his dad on Saturday.

The ministry time was taking longer than I had planned, and my sister was slated to be one of the last to receive ministry. I really wanted her to receive this final prayer ministry. We were moving into overtime, so during a small break, I ran through the sanctuary to the pay phones so that I could phone home to apologize and forewarn my husband that I would be late.

A young Italian pastor, Bruno Ierullo, from our church and his friend, who also looked Italian, were in my path. Bruno knew that I had just been in Italy, and he called me over saying, "Laurel! Come. I want you to meet my friend." I did not want to stop because I wanted to get to the phone and head off any family turmoil. We had a brief and polite exchange of, "Hello," and, "Nice to meet you." Then I excused myself as best I could to run and make my phone call.

I was still nervous about the amount of time I was at the church, so I was very anxious about the response that I was going to receive from my husband. To my surprise, Bob said, "No problem. We're fine. Take your time." I felt so much better, and then I immediately thought of Bruno and his friend. I ran back into the sanctuary to find them, but they were gone.

Then I felt terrible. So many people in Italy, from Sicily to Rome, had extended their warm hospitality to me in many ways. Yet when I had next met an Italian in my own country, I had been in too much of a rush to talk. I was not very impressed with myself. I went back into the group ministry session, and the time with my sister was amazing. It really helped her turn the corner in her life. However, I still felt disturbed with myself.

I went home and told my husband that I felt I had been inhospitable to the person that was with Bruno. I asked if we could either have them come for dinner or take them out for dinner because that was what so many Italians had done for me. He opted to take them out. So I phoned Bruno Saturday night, left a message with an offer of dining out, and waited. I got a response message saying that it would be wonderful. His friend was leaving on Monday. Therefore, he, his wife, Naomi, and his friend Matteo would have dinner with us on Sunday night. I thought, *Perfect!* We hired the babysitter, and it was all sorted out.

Matteo, Bruno, and his wife arrived at the house as we were getting Jack organized for bed. While I was upstairs, I could hear beautiful classical piano music. I came down to find Matteo at the piano. He obviously knew what he was doing, and he commented on the piano's nice sound. I was still commenting on his skill when our babysitter brought Jack in to say good night. I could see that Matteo was looking at Jack in a curious way. Jack was then taken upstairs.

As we prepared to go to dinner, I said to Matteo, "Our son Jack is a picture of the church."

He looked perplexed and said, "How so?"

My response was, "All the parts are there. They just don't work together." He asked Bruno if his interpretation was correct, and they nodded together.

We went to dinner nearby. Bruno sat at the end of the table with Matteo and me because all our conversations had to be interpreted, at least to some degree. At one point, Matteo said to me, "Do you know who I am?"

"No. Who are you?"

He replied, "I represent the one hundred and fifty million born-again, Spirit-filled, Charismatic Roman Catholics in the world to the Pope every Tuesday in the Vatican. I lead a congregation in the city of Bari, and I am a music professor in the university that is there." Inside I felt as if my jaw dropped down a few feet. I had had no idea, but I was intrigued. Then he said, "Your son, or the way you see your son, is a very interesting picture. I head up a ministry called United in Christ. Bruno works with me on it, especially in Canada. I have other people in England, the United States, and Brazil. You should come to some of our meetings. You must come to at least one. I think you will resonate with our mission." We agreed that would happen sometime in the future.

United in Christ continues as an anointed group of believers who facilitate the dialogue and unity among the many different expressions of Spirit-filled Christian and messianic churches and their leaders. I have loved their meetings and ministry. Today, I am on the board of directors for United in Christ, North America.

During our dinner, I told Matteo about my dream of Mel Gibson and spoke of my visit to Italy. I told him that when my friend and I were in Matera, I had a sense that the Lord wanted an orphanage and that somehow it was connected to Mel Gibson and my dream. Was it possible for the church to find Mel Gibson?

He said, "Of course! The Vatican can find him. And yes, there are orphans in Italy." The project did not proceed from there, but perhaps one day it will.

On my second Italian prayer-walk trip with my friend, we began with a church visit in Sicily. We then traveled up the boot of Italy to Matera, and ultimately, we flew out of Rome. As we settled into our seats and readied for our plane to takeoff, she informed me, with an amused smile, that she had told the Sicilian pastor we were visiting that I had extensive experience with women's ministry. As a result, he had booked me as a speaker for their women's night at their church. I was surprised and even mildly flattered, but I could feel my insecurities begin to rise. However, as I silently prayed, I knew that the Holy Spirit would be faithful.

I regarded it as a privilege to minister to the women in the Pentecostal church in Enna, Sicily. I spoke on the importance of the fifth of the Ten Commandments given to Moses by God on Mount Sinai for the people of Israel (see Exodus 20). The first four commands relate to our relationship with God. The rest relate to our relationship and behavior with other people.

The fifth commandment in Exodus 20:12 says, "Honor your father and mother that your days may be long upon the land which the Lord your God is given you" (NKJV). The family is established in scripture as a foundational and relational unit in society. It provides the love and the moral, instructional environment that is necessary for raising secure and God-fearing children, and ultimately, it undergirds our culture, which holds us together as a corporate collective.

Have you noticed how broken families often produce broken lives? Isolation, alienation, or lawlessness can easily be traced back to the family. We are called to honor and respect those who gave us life, whether they are good parents or not. That does not mean we can or should trust them or put ourselves in harm's way if they are abusive. Ephesians 6:3 teaches us that if we obey and honor our parents, we are promised that we will prosper and live long lives.

Another spiritual law is also at work. If we judge others, we open ourselves up to be judged in like manner. This aligns with the principle of sowing and reaping. There is also the spiritual law of increase involved with sowing and reaping. Obviously, our heavenly Father wants us to receive a multiplication of blessings and not curses. Obedience, honor, forgiveness, and mercy toward our parents and others will position us to reap the blessings of God's mercy, honor, and protection.

The Holy Spirit was there to help the women understand

why we did the very things that we hated when our parents did them. The things that we judge are seeds of sin that will continue to grow and manifest in and through us. This produces a harvest we do not want. Jesus instructed us to first remove the plank of sin from our own eyes (Matthew 7:5). Only then, could we help others see the speck of sin in their eye and become a helpful ministry resource to them.

I related my own story of judging my mother's flirtations. I had reaped the dark fruit of my judging her through my own flirting, early pregnancies, and terrible choices. In the church, we had a ministry time of repenting together for dishonoring our parents, judging, and subsequently walking in the same ways. I will add that sometimes, we behave in the opposite way, but it likely comes from the same root. Good parenting based on scriptural principles and modeling is so important.

Deuteronomy 6 tells us that fathers are to teach their children the principles of God when they walk, sit, and lie down. This instills a resident faith and lifestyle model within a child and prepares him or her to receive God's direction and blessings in life.

> Train up a child in the way he should go,
> and when he is old he will not depart from
> it. (Proverbs 22:6 NKJV)

Our heavenly Father teaches us how to successfully parent and illuminates the results that we can expect.

That day in Sicily during our ministry time of prayer, we repented, received forgiveness, and requested the Holy Spirit to empower us to walk in His ways. There were a few minutes of silence, and then one woman began to sob loudly. She ran up to me, fell on her knees, wrapped her arms around my waist, placed her face in my belly, and continued to sob. God bless her. At that moment, others began to cry, and the wailing and noise increased. I certainly learned that Italians are much more expressive emotionally than we North Americans are.

The pastor's wife looked alarmed and asked me, "What do you want to do now?"

Praise God that the Holy Spirit always has the answer. I said, "Sing a lullaby that you would sing to comfort and relax your children … in Italian, of course." She did this. The sweet presence of the comforting Holy Spirit began to fill the room as He brought revelation and healing to many. Wounds of childhood, which are caused or allowed by our parents can be deep. Sometimes they are buried and forgotten. They remain a dark filter that taints everything in our everyday lives. All that we go through personally can be brought to our Savior, who can and will heal us when we allow Him to bring His healing light and love to set us free. How awesome our God is!

Just before I left to fly back to Toronto, the news was full of accounts of a volcano that had erupted in Iceland. The debris in the air necessitated the cancellation of most flights. My Italian hosts were alarmed on my behalf. It was a long drive to Rome, and they were wondering if we should make the trip or try to rebook my flight at a later date. My friend wanted to remain in Matera for a while, so I would be on my own. I felt completely at peace and knew that the Lord would look after things.

As it happened, the only airline that was flying that day was Air Italia, which was the airline my friend had booked. That particular flight traveled over Spain instead of going on the more typical, northerly flight path toward Iceland and then Newfoundland, Canada. The airport was jammed with people trying to find alternate flights. Though Rome's airport can be confusing, I had no problem getting to the right gate and on the plane. The airport was full of angry, miserable people. On our large plane, there was not a single unoccupied seat.

After the muddled embarkation and some disputes over seat assignments, everyone settled down. I noticed that the younger woman beside me was tightly clutching her armrest with a white-knuckled grip. Obviously, she was anxious. I smiled and said, "Don't worry, we made it onto our flight, and we are on our way back home to Toronto."

With a tense voice and semi-clenched jaw, she muttered, "I'm afraid of flying."

I added breezily and with great confidence, "Really, don't worry. I am a lay pastor. My heavenly Father arranged for me to come here, and I am quite sure He will get me safely home. You're sitting beside me, so you will get there too." Then I added, "Would you like me to say a prayer for you and our safe arrival?" Perplexed but agreeing in her desperation, she shut her eyes tightly and listened as I prayed. Engines roared, and we began to move.

Safely in the air, she looked a bit dubious, but I could see that she was intrigued and thinking. After a little while, I turned on my movie screen, put on my headset, and began to watch. In those days with only a few movie choices available, everyone had to watch the same movie. The woman beside me fell asleep. About halfway through the movie, I started to laugh out loud at the comedy that was playing. It woke her up. She looked at me and then the movie and put her headset on. We both watched until the movie was over, chuckling in tandem over the funny parts.

When it was finished, she looked at me and said, "A miracle has happened. There is no way I could ever fall asleep on a plane. And there is no way I could watch a funny movie and laugh. Something has definitely happened. Thank you."

Curious, I asked, "Why are you flying then?"

She explained, "I have leukemia. My best friend is the only person who is important to me from my childhood that is still alive. She moved from our home in Germany because she married an Italian, and they moved to Italy. I wanted to see her before I die. I have two little children and a husband at home. My husband encouraged me and said I should do this."

I said, "You will be interested to know about something I learned from people who do a lot of prayer counseling. The spiritual root of leukemia is usually a person's deep-seated anger toward their father." Her eyes opened a little wider. "Does that fit?" I asked.

"Oh, yes," she said. "My father was very abusive."

I said, "Let's pray. I will lead you."

She forgave her father, who long ago had passed away. We asked the Lord to forgive her for dishonoring her father in her judgement and asked the Lord to cut off all the sowing and reaping that had come to her because of her sin of judging. Then we asked the Lord for her heart, blood, mind, and body to be healed.

She said, "You sound like two of my coworkers."

"Are they Christians?" I asked.

"Yes, they are born-again Christians. I was raised Catholic."

I said, "I would suggest that you spend a little more time with your coworkers and let them help you. God wants you well, and He wants your children to have and enjoy their mother."

She then added, "This is more of a miracle than even you know because I was supposed to be sitting on the other side of the plane. They were really having trouble getting a woman out of my seat, so they put me in her seat, which is here."

In the back of my mind, I thought, *Clearly, God had a divine appointment set up in advance for both of us.* As the flight continued, an announcement was made about extreme turbulence up ahead. I thought, *Oh, no. I do not want this to undo all the prayers that we have just prayed to remove her fear of flying.*

A picture of Moses standing at the edge of the Red Sea, extending his rod, and commanding the waters to part so that the people could walk through safely and escape their enemies flashed through my mind. In obedience to what I believe was a prompting from the Holy Spirit, I raised my hand, pointed forward, and quietly said, "I take authority over the wind, the air currents, the atmosphere, and everything it involves. I command you to come into peace and order. You will part so that this airplane can fly through without harm or turbulence in the name of Jesus Christ." To my surprise, the prayer had a more immediate effect than I had expected. There was no turbulence at all. It's a prayer that I pray almost all the time now whenever turbulence is announced on my flights.

I reiterate the importance of Romans 8:19–22: "Creation is groaning from the bondage of corruption ... and eagerly waits for the revealing of the sons of God." Creation needs us and our ministry. It awaits deliverance and redemption from the sin of mankind. As a follower of Jesus Christ who is filled with the Holy Spirit, I realized that I had a lot more authority than I had previously dreamed possible.

CHAPTER 9

More Mission Trips

I was invited to England to accompany the head of our women's ministry, Mary Audrey Raycroft. The plane trip was terrible. I had a single seat beside a noisy kitchen galley, the movie screen did not work, and the overhead light didn't work either. My seat was broken, it would not recline, and it was at a slight angle. To add to my discomfort, I had diarrhea, which was rare for me. When we got to England, the Lord said, *You are now empty. Stay that way for twenty-four hours.*

One of the events was a women's conference in a town near Newcastle. There were about three hundred women from all over the country. We had a young worship band the first evening, and the music was very loud and upbeat. In contradiction to the music, I could sense a sort of heaviness inside me, as if someone was grieving the Holy Spirit or something was oppressing the service. I heard Him say to me, *Get down*, which I knew meant, *Pray.* So in obedience, I got on my knees.

I was kneeling in the front row next to our leader, and I heard God say, *No, get down.* I knew that meant, *On your face*. I obeyed, and the moment I lay stretched out and facedown, an uncontrollable, spiritual travailing (weeping and groaning) came on me. It went on for about twenty minutes. When I got up, I could see a lot of perplexed faces, including my leader's face. I did not know how to explain it, so I did not try. I am sure some people thought that the problem was me, but I felt that it was deep intercession for someone or this particular event. We moved into the teaching, and everything was fine.

The next day, a session on ministry to women who had been victims of abuse, be it emotional, physical, or sexual, began. The various teams that had come were released at the end to minister to the women, and there were a lot of tears and prayer huddles around the room. I heard someone screaming above the rest of the noise, but it was on the other side of the auditorium, so I did not do anything.

Then a small group of people came and said, "Laurel, would you come? The men have taken a woman to the back room who is acting like an animal, and they do not know what to do." So I followed them to a small room in the back of the church, and in the corner on the floor, there was a woman who was fairly tall and very overweight. She did look like an animal as she snarled and made really strange sounds. I think it was because of the intercession that I had done the night before, that instead of being afraid, I was overwhelmed with compassion for her.

I went into the corner, got down on the floor, gathered her up as if she was a small child, started to rock her back and forth, and sang a song that I remembered my mother singing. These are the words: "Sometimes I feel like a motherless child, a long, long way from home." After a few minutes, she completely relaxed and began to quietly cry. Eventually, she calmed down. She got up, hugged me, thanked me, and left to join her friends. The meeting went on.

The Holy Spirit knows exactly what and how much is needed in every situation. Our job is to yield to His quiet inner promptings. The result is always awesome and often perplexing.

The next day, the room felt quite a bit lighter, but there still was an oppression that I could feel. The Holy Spirit said to me, *I want you to get up and start dancing to the worship music.* So I did: I started joyfully jumping around the front of the room, and again, I got some pretty strange looks (It's good to go away and minister because of the freedom that you have to be led by the Spirit and not be concerned about people's opinions). Then our leader prophetically said, "It's as if there is a cork in the bottle of a carbonated drink, and the Holy Spirit wants the cork to come out." She began to prophesy that it would happen to the women spiritually. In just a couple of minutes, one, then two, then more, and pretty soon, essentially the whole room was leaping and jumping in a dance line around the room. Joy had broken out and begun to spread. I was pretty impressed with the Holy Spirit.

Back home and several months later, my husband suggested that I go visit our third son in Germany, where he was studying in a business school exchange for one term. He and his father had taken a trip together, and this would be my turn to visit. Our son was busy with schoolwork, so I arranged to meet him for only three days, and then I would travel to Paris to meet with a girlfriend who was celebrating her birthday with her son, who was also studying abroad.

I arrived in Frankfurt and met my son. We were whisked off on the train to Oestrich-Winkel. It was a tiny village a few blocks long, surrounded by vineyards, and picturesquely sitting on the edge of the Rhine River. On arrival, he wanted us to dine at his favorite German restaurant and have a typical schnitzel dinner. The restaurant owner was very friendly and helpful, and the food was delicious.

We asked for his suggestions of short sightseeing trips for our next two days. His homey family restaurant had cartoon placemats on the tables featuring a map and important local landmarks. Using this simple map he advised, "Tomorrow, go to this promontory by train. Take the cable car up, and you will have a wonderful view of the countryside and the Rhine River. If you like, up near the top, there is an abbey that has a wonderful presence of the Lord. Go the other way the next day, and you will find one of the best remnants of a medieval castle."

I took the map back to the little room in an inn that my son had rented for me. I looked over the map a little more closely before bed. To my utter amazement and great delight, I saw that the church abbey that the restaurant owner had been referring to was established by Hildegard von Bingen. She was born in 1096, and she led a very impactful Christian life.

She might easily have been forgotten had it not been for feminist scholars. I learned a bit about her because of my art school experience and pre-Christian, feminist past. The artist Judy Chicago had put on an art event called the Dinner Party, which celebrated great women in history. In the show, Hildegard von Bingen was one the women who was greatly honored for the legacy that she had left. She was the tenth child in a merchant family, and when she was eight years old, she was dedicated as a tithe to the local abbey in Bingen, Germany. She went with her good friend, Jutta, who was a little bit older.

All the women in the abbey were there to serve the needs of the monastery in practical and spiritual ways. Jutta eventually became head of the abbey's women. At a very early age, Hildegard had visitations and communications from the Lord. In her later years, the heavenly songs, visions, and communications were written down by a friend who recognized their value. Hildegard's friend, Jutta, died in middle age, and Hildegard was chosen to take her place. Her spiritual sensitivity and wisdom had already been attracting attention and inquiries.

One day, the Lord told Hildegard to move the women across the river and set up an abbey of their own. For two years, Hildegard prayerfully and patiently waited for God's wisdom, strategy, diplomatic skills, and timing to get formal approval. The nuns at the convent were finally released to move and established vineyards to support their operations. My understanding is that they have been working the vineyards to this day. Hildegard became a voice of counsel to popes, princes, and all kinds of rulers. She was interested in both natural and spiritual healing. She was quite a proficient herbalist and an ambassador for the Lord.

In her sixties, she ventured forth into the public marketplace on preaching circuits through towns in Germany. This was extremely unusual in that day, but her message was anointed to resonate with and draw the common people to the Lord. She also exhorted church leadership in general to *come up higher* spiritually and embrace God's holy standard of conduct within the nation of Germany.

Of particular note were the heavenly choruses that Hildegard spiritually *heard*, then sang for a faithful recording scribe, and finally teach to the other faithful women in the abbey. Her music was reintroduced through feminist scholarship, and it is now recognized as the musical precursor to Gregorian chants. Hildegard had no musical training, but her ear was open to hear heavenly sounds and songs of praise and worship. She led a remarkable life and had an extensive influence.

My son and I set out as directed by the cheery restaurant owner and enjoyed the spectacular panoramic view of the countryside from the high promontory's elevation. We then began walking along the road from the cable car company to find Hildegard's abbey. We walked along an asphalt road for quite some time, seeing no cars or visible signs of civilization. We were surrounded by a forest. Lovely dappled light filtered down upon my son and me, as we ventured out on our quest.

It had begun as a pleasant walk, but subsequently, it continued for so long that we were starting to get discouraged and tired. Suddenly, a sweaty, heavy-breathing jogger appeared. I stopped him and asked in English for help to get to the abbey. He kindly responded in his broken, heavily-accented English that the abbey was actually still quite a long way off. We must have looked crestfallen. My cartoon map was obviously not to scale. To our great delight, he then offered to drive us there. So we took his kind offer and walked a little farther to his parked car. He then drove and dropped us off at the narrow beginning of the abbey's driveway.

Unfortunately, the abbey itself was closed to the public. Nonetheless, the tourist store was open. They had all kinds of books, local jams, their own wine, postcards, and other tourist items to sell. I didn't see what I was looking for, and I asked the nuns if they had any information on Hildegard herself. They were very excited that I knew who she was, and they proudly introduced me to a tiny little section with some CDs, books, and pamphlets about her life. I bought a good number of them and felt quite jubilant that we had finally been able to find this hidden Christian treasure in rural Germany.

Our walk home was much easier because we could see that the train station and town were directly below us. We only had to navigate down the hill and through multiple vineyards to get dinner and a train ride home.

Back at the inn, I marveled at God's goodness, journaled, and prayed a while. Before bed that night, I noticed that I had a little blister on my thigh and one on my ankle above my shoe. I prayed and wondered why they had appeared because there was nothing that could have rubbed against my skin to cause them.

After our final tour day, I continued on to Paris. The train ride through the countryside was a glorious tapestry of yellow mustard, green and blue flax, and lavender fields. My girlfriend and her son met me at the train station and gave me a whirlwind tour of Paris. They had both lived there before, so in three and a half days, I saw many of the important cultural and historical sites in and around Paris. Everywhere I went, I was quietly interceding and inviting the Lord to bring His presence and salvation to the people.

I could see and feel spiritual darkness over Paris, despite the physical beauty of the city.

By the time my airplane landed back home in Toronto, my feet were so sore, and I could hardly walk. They felt bruised, and I wondered what exactly what was going on. I wondered if it had been all of the walking that I had done. I should have taken more care to address physical warnings.

Three months later, my immune system completely crashed. Perhaps as I had been visiting and praying through the nations, I had unwittingly been stirring things up in the spirit realm that were bigger than I knew. Within about eight months, I had prayed in Italy, Israel, Germany, and finally in France. I still carried my prayer burden for Jack and the rest of the family and friends in my heart. I was so overburdened that I was getting spiritually soggy.

As our Christian school's chair of the board of directors, I knew that I needed to attend the students' Christmas performance. It was being held in a local church, which the school had rented. I quickly bathed and put Jack to bed. Because I was in a hurry, I took Bob's car. His car was in front and blocking mine in our driveway.

Once I was at the church, I carefully pulled very close to a wall near the front door. I assumed the church would be crowded with families, so I decided to leave my oversized purse in the car. I carefully tucked it in as far as I could, out of sight, beside the driver's door, and under the dashboard. My haste later proved to have been unwise. The Christmas service itself was wonderful. The students performed and sang with youthful enthusiasm while proclaiming the glorious birth of the King of kings, Jesus Christ. Afterward, we mingled, took photographs, and happily chatted. It was a lovely evening.

When I finally left the building and walked to the car, to my dismay, the driver's window had been smashed in. There were tiny bits of shattered glass everywhere, and my purse was gone. I was concerned for Bob's sake. It was his car, he had to drive it to work, and it was a very cold time of year. My own situation was also complicated because my purse, wallet, driver's license, credit cards, phone—everything—was gone.

However, what disturbed me the most was that a little book about Hildegard von Bingen was in the purse. I said, *Lord, I don't mind taking the time to have the car window fixed and to replace my credit and identification cards. I don't mind losing the cash, but I don't think I can easily replace that little booklet about Hildegarde Von Bingen. It is unlikely that I will ever be going back to the abbey in rural Germany. I really want that book back.* I sent up what I call a little flash prayer, which was really part of an ongoing conversation I was already having with the Lord. I left it with Him.

Four days later, our two middle sons came home from their out-of-town universities for the Christmas holidays. They did something that they had never done before. They stopped at a nearby small shopping mall and went into the Second Cup coffee shop. They sat down to chat, catch up, and have a brotherly Christmas coffee. The place was packed with people, who were also chatting and enjoying the pre-Christmas season.

While our sons were there, a woman about my age approached them and said, "You guys are probably the right age. I found this phone, and you might know how to open it or find the owner."

The two of them looked at it, and right away, our

younger son exclaimed, "That's Mom's phone! Where did you get this?" He looked in astonishment at the stranger.

She waved with her right hand at the street and said, "Behind the fire station, there is a little park. There is a purse there, and the contents are spread all over the ground. I only picked up the phone because I thought it might be valuable."

With many thanks, our two sons went as directed and collected all the contents. With great pride, they brought everything home. Of course, the cash and cards were missing, but my little book about Hildegard Von Bingen was there. There had been a four-day, hard freeze, which had preserved the book. The book was not in pristine condition but very close. Our sons then pondered the statistical probability of all the little connections that God had undertaken to bring the book back to me. We all enjoyed the incredible display of God's providence and His ability to answer prayer.

Shortly after that, I had a dream that was very simple and yet profound. I could see what looked like a translucent body with an outline of Jesus. I could see a similar translucent outline of me. However, I looked as I had when I had been between fifteen and seventeen years old. I was slim, and I had long blond hair. I can only assume that I was looking at my spirit. Jesus placed His hands over His heart and pulled them apart deliberately so that He could open up His chest like a flexible double wardrobe door. I knew that without words, He was saying to me, *Step inside.* I literally stepped into His body and turned to face forward with Him. He then closed His chest back up with me inside.

I woke up and pondered the scripture and seeming

reality of being *hidden in Christ*. He is within all believers by the Holy Spirit, but how much safer and more potent in the spirit realm can we be when we are hidden away inside of Him, where He can protect, impart to, and commune with us? It's pretty awesome. It gave me a new realization that whenever I laid hands on someone, they were also His hands. Wherever I went, I was going with Him, and He was going with me. As long as I stayed in Him spiritually, amazing things would happen. Signs and wonders could and would follow. Truly, the many wonderful things that happen are His works, which were designed and executed by the Author and Finisher of our faith.

Alternatively, problematic, unsettling things that happen are circumstances that are manipulated by the kingdom of darkness. It may be that our sin or disobedience is being used by the father of lies, who takes advantage of our ignorance and own ungodly desires and fleshly appetites, as well as those of our ancestors. Even geographical spiritual influences from past historical events may be combining to disturb, rob, and destroy our destiny and heavenly Father's family. Our salvation is a potent shield of protection.

In the beginning of my Christian walk, I learned to read scripture and pray it back out loud, literally word for word and even though I did not always understand its implications. Why? The Word of God is the incorruptible seed that always produces life (See Isaiah 55:11 and John 17:17). This was the case with Psalm 2, where God says, "Ask me for the nations." In childlike faith and obedience, I would often say, *Lord, I do not really know what this means or what it would look like, but I ask You to save the nations according to Your will and Your Word.*

As the years went on, revelation about that verse and many others would come during intercession and for my personal application. Sister Gwen Shaw's revelations helped me a lot because she had been a missionary, and she felt her life calling was to raise up other missionaries. We often prayed for specific nations in her meetings, and we were encouraged to do so on our own. I prayed for any nation that I had visited, according to the scripture, "Every place you put the sole of your foot, I will give you" (Joshua 1:3). The nations and different people groups are as beautiful and varied as the rest of His creation. He desires for everyone to know Him, His wonderful love, and His provision.

CHAPTER 10

Immune System Crash

During the summers, family and friends would come to spend some time together at our cottage. I also remember Conor's friend from school coming once. Elaine, her son, Jack, and I had a great time attending daily church, which primarily consisted of long sessions of happy, spirited worship. At that point, I was spending all summer at the cottage. It was too hard to bring Jack back and forth from the city to the cottage. He hated long drives because he would get overheated from being strapped tightly in his wheelchair.

Each summer, we were visited by a varied parade of people, both good and bad. I would try to find time to take my chair, Bible, and sun hat and sit on a rock at the edge of the water and pray. I always wanted to have somebody there at the cottage with me and Jack, just in case I fell or there was some kind of crisis. Our cottage was fairly remote and far from any neighbors.

When Jack was about sixteen years old, I found that the trek (carrying him along our rocky path and up and down the hill between the cottage and the lake) to be more and more physically challenging. Jack loved the water, but it was getting harder for me to offer him the cool freedom that he relished while floating and splashing in the lake. I don't think anybody other than his dad and I had the strength to manage his body.

That summer, I was edging into burnout. My skin was itchy, flaky, and cracked in many spots. Our family dog, Rusty, was obviously not feeling well. He whined at the door and frequently went in and out. Unfortunately, Jack then caught a cold. Whenever Jack was sick, he and I would be up all night. It was hard for him to relax enough to fall asleep at the best of times. I would sit on the floor in the bedroom with him over my lap. I would sing, listen to worship songs, pray, massage his back, and wait for him to calm down and fall asleep, often from exhaustion. I would carefully lift and place him on his mattress bed on the floor. That had been going on for several years.

One Friday afternoon after our visitors had left, we waited for my husband to arrive. To my surprise, he informed me that he was leaving the cottage the next day at noon. I said, "You can't. I'm not well enough to be here on my own. I don't have anybody else here. If you had told me, I would have arranged for my mom or sister to come."

He insisted, "I have been asked to speak at a small church group, and I am going." My heart sank. I knew that was a firm commitment.

After he left Saturday afternoon, I tried unsuccessfully to nap and became anxious. Early Saturday evening as I was bathing Jack, I could smell something pretty horrible. It smelled like sulfur. After laying Jack safely on the rug of the bathroom floor, I followed my nose. When I went into our bedroom between the bed and the sliding door, there was a horrible smell and creepy, dense presence. I instantly sprang into fear. Something demonic was right there. I think if I had been feeling better, I might have had the strength to bind and dismiss it, but that thought actually did not enter my mind. I was alone and afraid.

I put Jack to bed. By then, the smell was gone, but my fear remained. Throughout that night, Rusty wanted to go out five times. I could not just let him go loose outside for fear of the wild animals outside. Jack woke up three times in his discomfort, and he was snuffling in between. I finally took an oatmeal bath and then covered myself with lotion, hoping my itchy, irritated skin would calm down. I don't think that I slept at all.

The next afternoon, Elaine and Conor arrived for their scheduled visit. I explained my exhaustion and asked them to watch Jack while I tried to rest. I fell into a really deep sleep and felt much better for it. Sunday night was better as well. Monday morning, our extra help arrived. I was almost feeling back to normal.

Tuesday morning, I got up and noticed a couple of little watery blisters on my thigh. I thought, *How do you get a blister on your thigh?* I realized that I had little blisters like those during my visit to Germany.

Conor was studying nursing at university, so I asked him what he thought. He did not have an answer, but he said, "If it is not better tomorrow, you should probably have it looked at."

We prayed for healing and had a nice day, but by the next morning, little blisters were popping up all over my body. I could tell that I was getting a fever. So I decided. "Let's go. Sorry, but I have to go home." It was a long tortuous drive because Jack still was not 100 percent well.

Neither was I nor the dog. Once home, I took Jack into our swimming pool for an instant cool off and then lay down for a nap.

The blisters continued to enlarge and multiply, and the first ones started to break. The raw skin underneath became circles of inflamed flesh, which started to grow. When my husband came home, I left Jack with him and walked across the road to the hospital's family clinic. Our physician prescribed an allergy medication and some cortisol cream and sent me home.

When I got home and took off my sandals, to my horror, I could see that the skin under the straps had largely come off. Friday, my fever increased, and I sunk lower. I had no energy, and I knew that I was really sick. Our eldest son, who was then away at medical school, heard Bob's telephone report of my status. He was alarmed and insisted that I go to our hospital's emergency room. At that stage, I could not envision getting up to get into the car. That alarmed him even more. He wanted us to order an ambulance. Instead, Bob made an appointment with our doctor for the next morning. He first went in and told the family doctor how sick I was, and she expedited the process for me to see a dermatologist right away.

Elaine and Conor came to help. They guided my limp body into a borrowed hospital wheelchair, into the car, and then back into the wheelchair to get me to the hospital clinic. The dermatologist was alarmed. He called in every specialist and student available to see my skin, especially my back, and to observe my overall status. They took pictures and did two skin biopsies.

The young resident doctor carefully explained my prescription medication protocol. She wisely counseled,

"Don't look up this diagnosis on the computer. It will only frighten you. We are giving you a lot of drugs because we don't know what this is. We are guessing. But we are going to smack it with everything we have." There were four drugs: some heavy-duty painkillers, a unit of sixty milligrams of the prednisone, and two drugs to offset the side effects of the prednisone in my bones and my stomach.

The prednisone kept me awake twenty-three hours out of twenty-four. I took one painkiller, and I was so fuzzy that I could not pray or even think clearly, so I stopped taking them. I knew that the husband of our women's ministry leader was fighting lung cancer, and he was on ten milligrams of prednisone. Whatever they thought I had, I knew it was serious. I felt so terrible that I didn't have the curiosity or energy to research the diagnosis.

I heard the Lord whisper, *Don't call or speak to anyone.* I realized He was protecting me from speaking or hearing words that confirmed my sickness. He was present as my Healer.

At this point, most of my skin looked like raw meat. Fortunately, there was a heat wave. I had not previously realized how important my skin was in maintaining my body's temperature. I also learned that if I was in prayer, listening to worship music, or reading or speaking Bible scriptures—thereby sustaining the Lord's presence—I had no pain. Every moment became a quest to maintain this anointed place, which became my daily miracle. If I came out of His presence, I had lots of pain. That was my incentive to be a devoted seeker. In the day time, I would sit on our back deck in the heat and the sun like a rag doll, look at our garden, and pray. My clothes stuck to the oozing sores, so I needed to gently peel them off a couple times a day. I had an Epsom salt bath every morning and evening, where I watched the dead flesh come off and float around in the bathtub. It was disgusting. However, slowly my outer flesh started to dry, the sores stopped spreading, and the blisters stopped appearing. My skin started to heal.

Bless Conor's heart. He would come and softly dry brush my back to get rid of the bits of dry, dead skin hanging and catching on my clothes. I was not very hungry, but Elaine and Conor were determined to make sure that I was eating something nutritious every day. They also offered to play with Jack for a while each day and take him for a walk. All of this was happening while the End-Time Handmaidens and Servants convention was taking place in the southern United States. I had, of course, canceled my airplane flight and reservation. A couple of my friends at the Convention went on my behalf to Sister Gwen and said, "Please pray for Laurel. We think she is dying."

Unbeknownst to me on a Thursday morning, all the people at the convention were asked to focus their attention on my need and lift me up in prayer. Meanwhile as usual, I was limply resting on a deck chair at home on that still, hot morning. All of a sudden, I felt a breath or a kind of cool breeze blow over me. I was instantly energized. The shift was so dramatic that I immediately got up and watered the plants on the deck. That was a miracle! I knew that something had just happened. It wasn't until later that we made the exact convention prayer-time connection, but I was and still am grateful for God's mercy and answer to their corporate prayers for my healing.

When I went back to the hospital for a follow-up visit, the doctors were pleased with my progress. The biopsy revealed that I did not have any of the horrible diseases that they had been suspicious of. They did two more skin biopsies and instructed me not to lift Jack for six weeks. That was awkward. Over time and after the second biopsy's results, they dismissed all of their theories and gave me an allergy test on my back. In the end, they could only say that I had experienced an extreme allergic reaction to *something* and gave me a list of a hundred or so potential allergens. Even then, I insisted that while my immune system was currently suppressed, if I strengthened my immune system, my allergies would disappear. They did not agree, but it was a moot point, as I was getting better.

Meanwhile, our seventeen-year-old dog, Rusty, continued to have health problems. We found out from the veterinarian that he had a bladder infection, and he was given medicine. It did not help much. Then one day, a neighbor's dog attacked him and ripped open his belly. He had to be stitched up in the emergency veterinarian hospital and stay overnight. They reported their concern because he refused to eat or drink. I knew our family pet was dying.

Once home, Rusty improved a little with the medications and tender loving care, but one morning, the Holy Spirit said, *It is time.* Rusty was having a hard time going up or down the stairs. He was obviously suffering. I gathered up his bed and blankets and asked my husband to go to the emergency veterinarian hospital with Rusty and me. The doctors, who had been wonderful, came out and said, "We think it is time. We can give him more medicine, but it will not help much. His organs are failing."

So I said, "What do you do?"

"We'll put in an injection portal and a muscle relaxer.

You can hold him while we will give him the last injection. He may have some weird responses. Sometimes the bowels empty. Sometimes they vomit but sometimes not." They took Rusty away for a minute and brought him back.

Sitting on the floor, I put him on my lap. He was so sweet, snuggly, and totally relaxed. I thought, *Well the muscle relaxer did its job.* They came in, and I said, "You gave the relaxer to him?"

They said, "No, not yet. We just put in a portal." He was so calm that it was as if he was trying to help me be strong and accepting. I don't remember if they gave him the relaxer or not, but when they gave him the last injection, nothing changed. He didn't even twitch. I sat and cried as I pet our family dog. They left us alone for a while. Eventually they came back and gently said, "He is gone." They recommended cremation. Later, we buried his ashes at our cottage, the place where he loved to run, hunt, and bound about. Little did I know that this was a dress rehearsal that was preparing me for things to come.

CHAPTER 11

Jack's Graduation

Jack was nineteen and a half when the time was nearing for the end of his earthly life's story. I had finally recovered from my skin meltdown and had successfully rebuilt my health. I am grateful for that time, as I learned to stay very close to the Lord and continued to give particular attention to maintaining my own health.

I now believe that these experiences were part of a preordained preparation protocol. I got a telephone call from the End-Time Handmaidens' office in Arkansas. They wanted me to come down for an in-house teaching by a prophet named Pat Holloran. The urgency and insistence through one of their staff members that I come made me take note. I decided to go. In their subsequent meetings, the prophetic revelation and anointed presence of the Lord were exhilarating. Pat Holloran's humility and directness were unusual. There were less than fifty participants, including staff members, so we were privileged to have immediate and intimate access to this man of God.

In one of the sessions, I had a vision that looked like a heavenly throne room. Everything was fiery, colorful, moving and very noisy. It sounded like everything was breathing (almost roaring), and there were walls of fire that seemed to go on indefinitely. There was a huge Jewish marriage chuppah in front of me, but it was made of fire. Its four corners were towering, roaring, and shifting columns of fire. I wondered if these were angelic and fierce guardians. I could not see who was under the chuppah because everything had such a fiery brilliance. However, I could see myself in this scene. I looked like a tiny black dot, kneeling face down before the throne in fearful anguish and afraid to look up. I felt much like the prophet did in Isaiah 6. I could see and feel my flesh and filth in this otherwise holy and awesome place. The revelation intensified the fear of the Lord in me, and I remained determined to focus on and obey every leading and directive from the Holy Spirit of the almighty God.

When I got home from this prophetic conference, I had a dream. Our little women's prayer group was marching over the crest of a hill. It looked to me as if we were in Israel and surrounded by rocky outcroppings and scrubby growth. We could see below us a two-lane road, then a river, and then a town. We knew we were on a mission to go and evangelize the town with the gospel of Jesus Christ.

Suddenly, our attention was riveted. We heard noises that stirred up all kinds of fear. We heard snarling, snapping, growling, and barking. We were terrified. To our horror, we saw a pack of what looked like demonized wolves coming over the crest of the hill. We knew we were the target for their kill. My friends ran and scattered in all directions. Perhaps stupidly but reflexively, I froze into a fetal position on my knees and curled up in a ball. I cried out, "Jesus help me!" I could hear the horrible snarling noises getting louder. They were coming closer.

Against all reason, I peeked up and saw a line of intense, brilliant, and vertical light, which was about seven or eight feet high. Surprised, I lifted and turned my head to look a little more, just in time to see one of the wolves spot me and wheel around in my direction. Frantically, I thought, *Is this the end?* But then miraculously in a moment, the wolf transformed in nature and form and submissively crouched down in front of me. Then to my total amazement, the animal licked my hand. The aggressive monster that I had seen was suddenly behaving more like a well-trained pet dog.

I looked again at the light. It immediately expanded to the width of a large inviting door, and I woke up. *What was that all about?* I wondered. My heart was still pounding. I did what I always do when I have bad dreams. In my alarm, I began to pray, asking the Lord to undo the frightening events and any negative consequences of the dream, whether they were real or symbolic. I prayed for protection for everyone that came to mind, as well as other prayer needs, until I could fall asleep again.

When I got home, I busily prepared for Christmas. Our first grandchild, Emily, was born on December 23. Praise God for little girls! I made the long two-and-a-half-hour highway drive to see her that night. My daughter-in-law had a natural childbirth, and both baby and mother were in great shape. The new mother was tired, happy, and very hungry, but it was well past the hospital dinnertime. Therefore, our son and I went out to find a really good restaurant that he knew about, and we brought back a celebratory roast beef dinner to the hospital.

We stopped briefly at their home to return some things that she no longer needed, but when we got back into my car and I turned the key, the engine started making, "Chug-chug-chug," sounds and then stopped running. *That's odd*, I thought. It had never happened before. I tried it again, and it did the same thing.

My son said to me, "We are taking my car. Let's get this dinner to the hospital and deal with your car when we get back."

Several hours later when we returned to the town house, the car's condition was still the same. We agreed that I would stay overnight, as it was now very late and the highways were dark and deserted. We would go directly to a dealership in the morning. After calling home, I fell into a deeply, restful sleep. The next morning, the mechanic made it clear that the car problem was not very complicated. He believed that as long as I stayed on the highway, I would be fine. He noted that at low speeds and stop-and-start junctures, I might have a problem with stalling. I needed a minor belt replacement, which they did not have in stock. It was now daylight, so I was willing to try to make the drive home to our own mechanic. Everyone was notified by phone and given an update on when I expected to be home.

Christmas Eve was upon us. A lot of things that I had planned to do remained unfinished due to my prolonged visit to see our first grandbaby. Before the drive home, I asked the family to do their best to decorate the Christmas tree that I had already purchased and put up in the living room. They also needed to get Christmas Eve dinner ready. In the end, I am delighted to report that it was the most relaxing Christmas Eve I have ever had. I arrived home not long before dinner.

Jack was annoyed with me, and he had been for a few months. Part of the problem was that well-meaning staff members at his school kept asking me, "What are you going to do with Jack now that he is nineteen?" It annoyed me that they would speak this way in Jack's presence, but there is no law against insensitivity.

After Christmas, the baby was brought to be introduced to the family. Jack seemed unimpressed and perhaps a bit jealous. He had become used to being my primary focus.

Days later, on January 13, 2013, I received word that Sister Gwen Shaw had graduated to her heavenly home. She had passed on to heavenly glory, surrounded by people that she loved at Engeltal, in her own bed at home. Apparently as she looked startled and at those around her, her last words were, "Are you ready?" Sharon Buss, the current leader and president of Global Outpouring (formerly End-Time Handmaidens and Servants), told me that with the intensity of those words, she was so convicted that she was almost checking to see if she was still saved. There was that much urgency in Sister Gwen's last words and challenge.

In honor of their dear friend, Sister Gwen, the ministry was planning on having a thirty-day celebration of her life, with open meetings every morning and evening, which would be broadcast each of those thirty days. Great saints and friends came from all over the world to the ministry base in the Ozark Valley, Arkansas, to honor her influence and memory. Their dates and times to speak or preach were all scheduled. At home, I silently wished that I could be there. Of course, it was impractical.

About a week later, I had a vision. It was a flash of a mental picture in the middle of the day. I saw Jack perfectly healed, normal, and sitting at the bottom of a short flight of stairs. The stairs were wide, low-rise, and made of white marble. They looked like they were going up to a throne. Jack was sitting on the bottom step, leaning back on one elbow. His head was thrown back, and he was laughing hilariously aloud. He was obviously filled with joy and feeling completely free. The vision was very inspiring. I wondered, *Lord, would you do that for him?*

A few days later, Jack got a bit of a cold, and I kept him home from school. He liked staying home. In his earlier years, he and I enjoyed going to school, but it was different now. He was reluctant. I believe as he aged, the cuteness factor had worn off, and he was not receiving the same attention and devotion that he had previously experienced. Also, the question of what would happen with Jack's care after his school years were finished hung unanswered in the air.

On Wednesday, January 31, I hosted our regular small group of women intercessors for a morning meeting. Jack loved these women, and they loved him. Imelda, who had been our faithful helper for over nineteen years, sat with Jack, less than eight feet away in our attached family room. Imelda commented later on how quiet he was as the meeting progressed. As we sang in worship and prayed, we became aware of and commented on the intense and frankly wonderful presence of the Lord in our midst. I wondered, *Lord, why? Do you want to do something? Do you want us to pray something? We honor You and will do anything that You want us to do.* After our worship and prayer time, we just enjoyed His presence. What an awesome God we serve. It was a much-needed preparation for me, given what was to come.

Everyone left, and Jack had his lunch. Then as usual, he lay on his floor mattress with its colorful, plastic bed guards that kept him safely contained. For forty-five minutes, he listened to a Christian CD of quiet soaking music. He loved this daily routine during his rest time. The house was quiet. Only the soft music drifted through the house through the monitor that was in his room. Imelda and I were both in the kitchen.

At the end of the CD, she went upstairs and shattered the calm in the household with her scream. I ran upstairs. Jack was lying very still, and he had turned a deep-blue color. I wondered if he was dead. I grabbed his body and began mouth-to-mouth resuscitation. I put some cold water on his face, gave him a few cheek slaps, and in between breaths, told Imelda to call 911. Because we live across the road from a big teaching hospital, the ambulance arrived very quickly. The paramedics came in and checked Jack's pulse. One of them looked at me kindly and said, "It's very weak."

I thought, *Is it there or is it weak? Is the paramedic being kind by lying?* They loaded Jack and me into the ambulance. I quickly texted our family: *Jack's in trouble, not breathing, going to the hospital, please pray.* We drove into emergency bay, where the staff moved very quickly and efficiently. Jack was hooked up to all kinds of machines, and all kinds of medical efforts were being made on his behalf.

When the emergency room doctor came out to speak to me, I asked if he would speak with our son who was in medical school. Looking back, I think that my request intensified the medical intervention efforts by the emergency personnel. My son spoke to the doctor. Then my son said that he was coming as fast as he could (a two-and-a-half-hour drive). My text to the family had produced quick results. One son flew in from New York City. Another son and Jack's dad drove up from their respective downtown businesses. It was a very intense time.

I did not want to see anyone, and I felt conflicted about what I should do. I was trying to press in to ask the Lord whether I should be praying for resurrection life or healing. I was not getting any answer. It was very distressing, and yet in some way, there was an inner calm. I prayed specifically in English in the best way that I knew how and in my spiritual language the rest of the time. Praying in unknown tongues is one of the nine gifts of the Holy Spirit. It enables us to connect with our Lord and His will without engaging our intellect or mind. It is a potent gift that brings strength and refreshment. It often enhances spiritual hearing and produces other amazing results.

When our eldest son arrived, he confirmed what I thought. He showed me that the IV liquid dripping into Jack was beginning to bloat his abdomen, indicating that his organs were not working. The end was upon us. I surprised myself when I calmly said, "Well then, let's turn the machines off." My eldest son then began to plead with me to wait for his wife to come. She had already left with their new baby, and his wife's dad was driving her in. She wanted to be with us. So we waited. During that time, we agreed to let each family member have his or her own private time with Jack. I had read that science suggests that hearing is the last sense to go, so we all took turns and entered into our goodbye time alone with Jack in our own personal ways.

The nurses were wonderful, and eventually, they moved us from the emergency room to a quieter critical-care room on a different floor. When the whole family had arrived, we all gathered around. Our third son played the song "Amazing Grace" on his phone, and we sang along as best we could. Then he played a song that he knew I loved, from the television series *Touched by an Angel*. In one particular episode, a mother sings a song that she wrote before her son died. The line that always stood out for me was that in spite of her son's death, she could sing, "As long as I shall live, I will testify to love." I believed that she meant the power of Christ and His love was sufficient to hold and strengthen us in any and every situation.

We then asked that the machines be turned off. They had forewarned us about all kinds of upsetting physical things, which often happen at death. Our family dog's passing helped me. I rebuked and broke the power of their words. I asked the Lord to make sure that no fleshly upset would manifest and that Jack would go from us to Him with no interference. I expected the same kind of peace that I had seen with Rusty, and the Lord answered my prayer. He did not even flinch. It was a beautiful, peaceful transition. I am eternally grateful for that kindness.

As everybody slowly began to gather his or her things to go, and I said, "I need to stay here through the night." They were not surprised. Through the years of Jack's life whenever he was sick or distressed, we would spend the night awake together. This would be our last one. I asked my husband if he would come and pick me up in the morning.

Again the nurses were wonderful. They were obviously moved by the whole event, and they agreed to my staying with Jack, as the unit was not very busy. As I sat with him, I thought of the *Pieta*, Michelangelo's statue of Mary holding the body of her crucified son, Jesus. Jack was my son, but he had also been a vehicle of my salvation. Jack, whose Christian name was John, had been my John the Baptist. His life and death had pointed out the One who purchased my salvation, the Lamb of God, Jesus.

The Lord gave me some scriptures. I had been resourceful enough to take my Bible.

> Then those who feared the Lord talked to each other, and the Lord listened and heard them. A scroll of remembrance was written in His presence concerning those who feared the Lord ... they will be my treasured possession. (Malachi 3:16)

> But to you who fear my name, the Sun of Righteousness shall arise with healing in His wings ... you shall trample the wicked ... behold I send you Elijah the prophet, before the great and dreadful day of the Lord, and He will turn the hearts of the fathers to the children and the hearts of the children to their fathers, lest I come and strike the Earth with a curse. (Malachi 4:2–6)

I felt that the Lord said, *I am here. Remember there is the ultimate healing in Jesus.* I was reassured that before the great day of the Lord's return, the spirit of Elijah, John the Baptist, and those who proclaim the good news will emerge in power to restore fathers, children, and the family and to bring His kingdom to the earth. I believe those days are now upon us.

As I sat with Jack's body through this last night, I asked the Lord, *Should I be praying for resurrection? Should I be doing something I am not doing?* I heard a quiet voice say, *I showed you where he was.* Immediately, the vision of Jack laughing at the foot of the heavenly stairs to the throne flashed through my mind, followed by the dream of him skiing up the mountain. I realized that in both cases, I was seeing him in heaven. He was happy, and he wanted to be there. That brought me great comfort in the midst of my anguish.

In the night, I was able to ponder the meaning of life and how one broken and short life can have such a profound impact on so many. I was really grateful that Jack had not died a slow, lingering death. I realized that the situation, in many ways, was God's mercy, both to Jack, who was surely quite happy to be in heaven, and to me because I did not have to watch him suffer. In fact, I did not see him suffer at all. We had both had more than enough of that. Interestingly, I found it especially easy to forgive anyone and everyone who had hurt me or my family in any way. The offences now seemed so trivial.

My husband came at daybreak, and he brought some clothes for Jack with him. We then went together with his body down to the morgue. We made a prayerful request to the man that was receiving him and his clothes. We did not want anyone touching him other than to dress him. He quietly nodded, and we left.

I was in an anesthetized state for a number of days. I was sad but not overly so because I was aware of the

Lord's presence. It felt like I was protected in a cotton cocoon. Fortunately, my husband was not in the same place. He was moved to action. He called our church pastor to come and speak to us about funeral arrangements. Bob suggested that we hold the service in the same funeral chapel where a recently deceased friend of ours had just been celebrated.

I quipped, "Don't you think that place is way too big?" The funeral that we had attended had been for a well-known football hero who had become a chaplain and a minister in his latter years.

Bob said, "No, I think Jack touched a lot of lives, and I think you'll be surprised." I was not totally sure about that, but I really did not care enough to comment one way or another. I was just glad he was looking after it. I was numb.

Bob told our sons that they each had two and a half minutes to speak at the funeral. He would show a DVD of family pictures, and I too had a three-to-five-minute time slot if I wanted it. I did not think I would or could speak. Then the Lord began to talk to me in a mind picture. He showed me wearing a white pantsuit that He had instructed me to buy years ago, before I went to the Ottawa prayer breakfast and when I was a new believer. I knew instantly that He was saying, *Wear that to the funeral.* Obviously, a white pantsuit was unusual attire and not the typical somber dress for a funeral. I could see His point because His saints are scripturally depicted as wearing white garments of righteousness in the spirit realm.

The evening before the funeral, I felt the Lord say to me, *I want you to speak and tell everyone how Jack died.* I realized that He wanted me to share that his exit was relatively benign. That would stop any worldly theories that demeaned or slandered the Lord, His love, and His care. Everyone who knew me knew that I believed in and ministered healing prayers. Our enemy, the devil, could easily twist these times and events as an invitation for the mockers to speak, unless I set the record straight.

The morning of the funeral, I finished writing out what I wanted to say. I also asked Jack's school music teacher and Elaine to sing a couple of Jack's favorite songs. That was very special. One song was "Let's Go Fly a Kite," and I felt like Jack's spirit had flown away to heaven like a kite, flying and bounding without a string. I did my best to relay the hope that is embedded in the gospel, both here and in eternity.

Then our pastor, Steve Long, got up to speak and said that he had asked me how evangelistic I wanted him to be in his funeral address. My response had been, "I want my neighbors and my family to know the love of Jesus. You say whatever you feel led to say." He proceeded to tell the story of Mephibosheth, the disabled son of Jonathan, David's covenantal friend. Years later after Jonathan had died, David became king. He enquired whether any offspring of Jonathan were alive so that he could bless them. He learned about Mephibosheth and his life as a disabled man. True to his heart's intent, King David invited Jonathan's son to live with him in the palace and eat at the king's table.

King David is a picture of Jesus, and the pastor's analogy was illuminating. He quickly explained the good news of the gospel and reaffirmed that I desired that people would know the Lord. He invited all people attending who wanted to know Jesus or reaffirm their faith in Him to repeat a prayer. It sounded like almost everyone said what I knew was the "Sinner's Prayer." which I had said myself so many years earlier. Afterward, many people talked to me about that moment in the funeral service. Even in death, Jack's life was witnessing, speaking, and wooing people to Jesus.

After the funeral and our family's time together was over, I found myself alone in the house for the first time in many years. People kept telling me that I should let myself cry. I thought that sounded reasonable. I took my Bible, some water, and a box of tissues and went upstairs with the intention of lying on Jack's bed and crying. My head had not even touched the pillow as I was starting to lie down when I heard the Lord say, *Go to Engeltal*. It was so clear that I got right back up, and I was surprised. I went downstairs and got on the computer to see if I could find flights to Arkansas so that I could join the thirty-day celebration of Sister Gwen's exceptional life. I saw that I could fly out the next day.

I phoned my husband to say, "Could I do this for a week?" because I knew that Sister Gwen's convocation and life celebration was still going on.

Bob said, "Sure, go ahead."

I phoned the office at Engeltal and spoke with our new leader, Sharon Buss. Right away, she said, "Oh, yes, come. We will look after you," which indeed they did.

When I arrived at the airport in Little Rock, a man who lived at Engeltal picked me up. I knew his wife had recently died of a brain tumor. He and I spoke a lot about grief, being a Christian, and the day-to-day realities of missing a loved one. It was a mutually comforting conversation. I do not think that we have talked that much since then because he is naturally a quiet man, but a deep, grateful, and loving bond remains because we were able to openly share our mutual grief and pain.

To my delight when I got to Engeltal, my sleeping arrangements were not what I had expected. They did not put me in the women's dormitory, where I had slept several times before. They had given me my own room on the second floor of a house with one of the staff members, Linda Gladman. Every morning, my bedroom would fill with golden light as the sun rose, and I could look out over the beautiful Ozark Valley and Mountains. It was glorious! When I got up, Linda would offer me tea or coffee, throw some bird seed outside of her sliding-glass back door, and then worship and sing songs that she had written.

One of them was about hugging the cross because even though he was wounded, Jesus hugged the suffering of the cross to fulfill His Father's will. Her song noted that we could too. We should not allow our human, fleshly nature to pull us away from embracing unpleasant times and the Lord. We can always look to Jesus, who desires to comfort us in all our difficulties, leaving us free to love Him, ourselves, and others. As she sang, I listened and watched the beautiful birds gobble up the seeds scattered outside her glass door. It was a very therapeutic place to be.

The meetings themselves were wonderful. The first evening, Don and Catherine James were ministering. I do not remember what they talked about, but afterward, I went and asked them for prayer, telling them what had happened. As a couple, they enveloped me and ministered to me for quite a long time.

After three or four days, I called home, and Bob said, "Why not just stay until the end of Sister Gwen's life celebration? It's only a few more days." That meant I got to be there and participate for the last ten days. On the last day, a drizzling, freezing rain started. They told everyone that the last meeting would be held in the valley where they all lived, instead of up on the highway in their big meeting room. They advised that people not try to come down the long steep gravel road into the valley, which meant that most people would not come at all. It became a very intimate meeting with a delegation from Africa honoring the impact that Sister Gwen had had on their lives, ministries, and nation. It was a tender, joyful event. Afterward, everyone went outside to see the fireworks that would gloriously close the thirty-day convocation. I actually watched from inside Linda's home through her glass door. Outside it was cold and wet, but the fireworks were exciting, colorful, shiny, and lovely.

At dawn, an appointed driver came to Linda's home to take me to the airport. To my delight, the freezing rain had created a world that was visually spectacular. Every blade of grass, branch, and weed had a thin coating of ice on it. The roads were absolutely dry, but all the vegetation was encased in what looked like glass. The whole earth seemed to shine in the rising sunlight like an illuminated crystal palace. It was truly heavenly. As we drove closer to the city of Little Rock and the sun strengthened, the ice disappeared. My memory felt like a gift from God.

After arriving home, every once in a while, a little tear would come to my eye, but that was all. The Holy Spirit reminded me, *We do not mourn as the world does.* First Thessalonians 4:13–18 says,

> But I do not want you to be ignorant, brethren, concerning those who have fallen asleep, lest you sorrow as others who have no hope. For if we believe that Jesus died and rose

again, even so God will bring with Him those who sleep in Jesus … For the Lord Himself will descend from heaven with a shout … And the dead in Christ will arise first. Then we who are alive and remain will be caught up together with them in the clouds to meet the Lord in the air. And thus we shall always be with the Lord. Therefore, comfort one another with these words. (NKJV)

The following spring and summer were very cool, so thankfully, we had very few guests at the cottage, be they family or friends. The first time that I was alone at the cottage and Bob had gone back down to the city to work, I decided that because it was six months since Jack's death, perhaps it was time to try to have that big cry that I had not yet had. I again took my Bible, my water, some tissues, and a hat and went down to sit on the rock by our lake. Almost immediately, a mother duck jumped up out of the water onto the edge of the gray-and-pink granite beach, which was only a few feet away from my chair, and looked at me expectantly. Although this was unusual, we stared at each other, and I said to her, "Okay, just a minute. I'll go get you some bread." I quickly made the trek up our steep hill, which I had carried Jack up and down in my arms so many times before. I then collected some healthy bread for the mother duck and the little babies that I had seen coming behind her. Once the babies could see their mother happily eating the bread, they came and joined in the feast.

After their big meal, they all settled down about a foot away from my feet on the rock. In all of this, I began to notice that the mother was limping. I could see that one of her ankles above her webbed foot had some sort of tendon poking out. She had obviously been damaged somehow, be it a predator or circumstances. I had an aha moment! She was a picture of me: a wounded mother who still had three little fluff-ball babies that needed to be looked after. I too was wounded, and my heart had been broken, but we still had three sons for whom we were responsible. I needed to make sure that they were cared for and watched over physically and especially spiritually. I heard the Lord say to me again, *We do not mourn as the world mourns.* My heart settled, and I quietly agreed with the truth of His Word.

I fully expect to see Jack again in my future heavenly home, but I knew then that I still had important family responsibilities to fulfill on Earth. The day was getting late, and the ducks were still settled quietly at my feet. This was starting to concern me. They were very exposed on the open rock. I blessed them and pleaded with the Lord to watch over them through the night. *Please, Lord, keep them safe from foxes, weasels, and any other predator that might be out hunting tonight.* I went to bed still feeling concerned, but I tried to entrust their care to the Lord.

In the early morning, I jumped out of bed and went to see if they were there. They were not. That alarmed me a little bit, and I said, *Lord, please.* I took my bread and other things down to my chair. To my great delight and in less than an hour, there they were, happily paddling toward me once again, and we spent another day together. I took a picture of the ducks and sent it to my family. I informed them, "You will not believe it. You know I love to pray healing prayers, but now I am praying for a wounded mother duck and her three fluffy ducklings." I chuckled to myself and asked the Lord, *Who am I really praying for? The duck or me?* It did not matter.

As the days went on with my new family of ducks, I guess the word got out in the bird world that there was food at our cottage, and a few more aggressive ducks showed up. They would try to chase my new bird family away. I was impressed with myself. All I had to do was stand up, and the aggressors would retreat. It was a new lesson in spiritual authority. I would feed the mother and babies, and then, I would feed the other ducks off the end of the dock, which was farther away. That worked well. Our routine kept us all happy.

Later around what would have been Jack's twentieth birthday, I sent the family another phone picture with a message, which read, "My congregation has grown. We have twenty-eight ducks!" I was slowly healing, but I knew that I would miss this quiet time in our Canadian country cottage with the ducks.

In Jack's lifetime, a great many of the best ministers and healing evangelists had laid hands on and prayed for him (Randy Clark, Mahesh Chavda, John and Carol Arnott, Benny Hinn, Billy Burke, Reinhard Bonke, and Gwen Shaw). I realized that no man or woman could do what only God could do. We could all be messengers of His truth and the good news of the gospel and conduits of His presence.

Healing is part of our Father's provision. I think that's important because there are many people, who when confronted with a Christian dying, will say, "Well that healing prayer did not work." Beloved, God has purposes that we cannot fathom. He lovingly works all things together for our good, although we often only recognize it later. It's very rare for us to understand the storm of the circumstances that we are in unless we can get His perspective or take time with Him to look back. That is the reason that we need to have faith in His good intentions and love.

I realize that if Jack had been healed, my entire life would have been focused on developing him, body, soul and spirit, so that he would grow, be educated, and lead a productive life. Because he is now no longer in his earthly body, I am free to minister as the Lord leads. After Jack's passing, my heart's desire has been to lighten the sorrow and trouble that so many endure and to help them enter into the Lord's rescue plan for this life and eternity. After Jack's death, I was able to go on mission trips usually twice a year. I learned a lot. I had some great experiences. Sometimes, I preach, but I always minister. It has been a very exciting and gratifying time.

CHAPTER 12

Hope and Inspiration

As the summer came to a close, I heard the Lord ask me, *Are you and I okay?* I knew that He knew the answer. He just wanted me to know the answer. Yes, Lord, we are okay. I don't blame You in any way, and I do believe Jack is now free and enjoying his new heavenly life. Thank You also for his quick and peaceful graduation. I am eternally grateful for all You have done for me and my family, and I thank You for Your kind love and comfort."

After that summer, I went home wondering how I would manage real life again. God apparently had a plan. To my surprise in early September, one of the leaders of United in Christ phoned to ask, "Would you come and minister in our leaders' school of ministry? We would like you to teach on the mother heart of God and be a small group leader at our retreat near Rome." I would go from ministering to ducks to Rome. Under normal circumstances, that would have excited me, but I was feeling very tentative and unsure. I told him that I would get back to him.

Bob came home from work, and he informed me that John Arnott, the senior pastor of our church, had asked if

Bob and I would like to go to the leaders' school of ministry near Rome. I realized that God was saying, *You can both go together. It's time to reenter church life and ministry.* Praise God for ministers who help us along in our healing journey.

The October leaders' retreat in Italy was a wonderful experience. In many ways, reentering ministry was like a duck going into water; it was easy to swim again. I facilitated the ministry of a small group of women, whom I grew to love. The Holy Spirit also made sure that I received ministry. During the prophetic teaching, the woman in charge asked us to give a biblical name to our spouse or neighbor, as a prophetic *calling out.* We would impart a dimension of destiny with our words and name choices, as we were led by the Holy Spirit.

Bob looked at me and said, "Ruth."

I was a bit surprised, but I thought, *Ruth ultimately marries Boaz, who was a type of Jesus, and that is a good thing.* She was a Moabite and not a Hebrew, but she remained faithful and loyal to Naomi, her Jewish mother-in-law, and to the Lord. Naomi is a picture of Israel and the Jewish people. While living in a foreign land, Naomi was widowed, and both of her married sons died. Only Ruth, her foreign-born, Gentile daughter-in-law remained faithful and loving toward her mother-in-law through all things.

Because of a widespread famine, the two women returned to Naomi's hometown and people in Bethlehem. Ruth worked diligently in the fields and provided food for herself and Naomi by gleaning the leftover bits of grain that were left by the harvesters. In a divinely ordained meeting in the barley fields, Ruth met Boaz, a wealthy landowner and distant relative of Naomi's family. Naomi instructed Ruth with God-given wisdom in her dealings with Boaz.

Their courtship and marriage was the result. The new couple bore a son who became the grandfather of Israel's great King David and ultimately Jesus. God always has a plan, and He had a plan for me.

I found my prophetic name of Ruth and the Bible story comforting. I remembered that Jesus was my Boaz. He supernaturally redeemed me, watched over me, and was committed to provide for me as Boaz did for Ruth. Father God always has a plan for our good and not for evil.

In the prophetic teaching, we were then instructed during the ministry time to ask the Holy Spirit to take us back to a word, dream, or a vision that we believed He had authored. The teacher then asked the Holy Spirit to lead us and expand something that He had prophetically given to us in the past. Immediately, I thought of my dream where vicious wolves attacked us as we marched through Israel. In the dream, the presence of the Lord Jesus Christ became my refuge from danger and provided an open door of light. When that happened, the wolves were immediately tamed and subdued. In that moment, I remembered the Holy Gospel's words in the book of John 10:9, where Jesus declared, "I am the door. If anyone enters by Me, he will be saved, and will go in and out and find pasture."

Obviously, the Holy Spirit was inviting me to go through the opening of light. As I did, a vision began. I was instantly dressed like a biblical Ruth, with a threadbare, neutral-colored dress and a shawl over my head and shoulders. Because our ministry room was cold, I had worn a shawl that day. In the vision, the light on the other side of the door was so brilliant that it took time for my eyes to adjust. When they did, all I could see was an endless field of ripe wheat.

Boaz approached me as what I assume was a

personification of Jesus. He said to me, "Hold out your shawl." He poured a large amount of threshed grain into the thick, course fabric of the shawl that was over my arms and said, "You will reap where you have not sown." Clearly, evangelism was somehow part of the Lord's plan for my future. I felt reassured of His supernatural, abundant provision. Everyone in our leaders' school of ministry and United in Christ Italy finished our trip with sightseeing and fellowship. Having enjoyed it all, Bob and I returned home.

About a year after our trip to Italy (and about a year and a half after Jack's graduation to heaven), I woke up one Sunday morning, saw the letters, and heard a voice within saying, *Reims*. I wondered if it was a city as I prepared for our home church. Because he was young and more technologically oriented, I asked Conor, who immediately looked it up on his phone. As he searched and read aloud his findings, we learned that it was a city in France and that Joan of Arc had once adamantly demanded that the dauphin cross over enemy lines to Reims to be crowned and anointed as King. That intrigued me. We found many more interesting historical details. I realized that I had booked an upcoming mission trip with World Missions Alliance to Ireland but that it was an open-ended airline ticket. I had hoped that my husband would join me later. I could easily add a trip to Reims at the end of my itinerary. After consulting with my husband, we agreed that I would visit France for three days and then fly home from Paris instead of Dublin.

I learned that Reims was considered by many to be the spiritual heart of France. I visited many tourist sites and museums in this ancient city. It was easy to traverse on foot. The city had begun as the most-northern

Roman army headquarters. They excavated limestone for construction of this once-great city, leaving over seven miles of underground tunnels. These tunnels provided a safe hiding place for the early Christian missionaries and subsequent religious orders over the centuries. Today, these tunnels continue to be used for storage by the most-famous champagne producers in France.

Clovis, who was a Germanic lord and king and reigned in 496 AD, was an exceptional leader. He was married to a Christian princess from Burgundy, in what was probably a political alliance. She had tried to explain the gospel and the superiority of the Lord Jesus Christ to him. He remained true to his Germanic gods, until one fateful day.

He was in a battle, and for the first time, he risked losing to his enemies. He cried out to the Lord in his desperation. He declared that if the God of his wife was true and he won the battle, he would worship at the higher altar of Jesus Christ. The battle suddenly turned, and he was victorious. On his return from the battle, the bishop of Reims discipled and water baptized him. A few thousand of his men followed suit. From that day forward, virtually every king in that European area went to Reims to be crowned, to be spiritually anointed as king, and to receive a mantle of authority to rule under God.

In keeping with this history, the Holy Spirit spoke to Joan of Arc and insisted that the dauphin cross enemy lines to be crowned king in Reims. There are many more historical details that enlarge upon this theme. In World War I, the Germans flattened Reims during their bombing. I believe that the devil knew this city was the spiritual heart of Christian authority to rule in France. In World War II, the people of Reims did not want their beautiful, rebuilt, and art-deco city smashed again, and they let the Nazis come through easily.

Today Reims is a very secular university town, as well as the center and home of the champagne industry. We now know that the temperature and humidity within the miles of the ancient tunnels is perfect for the storage of wine in general and champagne specifically. The early Christian monks were noted for their excellent wine, and its sale financed their endeavors over many years.

The Holy Spirit instructed me to take bread and wine communion elements to four historical and spiritual sites in Reims and pray for healing and restoration. I went to the cathedral, the basilica, Palace Tau (the grounds of the first Christian abbey), and finally, the grounds of a champagne house, which still provides tours of the early monks' underground chapels and areas where they hid from roving barbarian hordes and enemies. When I had finished, I felt Him ask me to pray that the spiritual heart of France would beat again. With my part of this mission accomplished, I went home and continued to pray for France. My awe of God's ability to strategically lead and direct His people expanded exponentially. Nonetheless, life was often natural, real, and raw.

Like most couples, my husband and I had been through a lot in our marriage. Besides the grief of Jack being gone, issues still brewed under the surface. Sometimes I would feel that he was trying to start an argument. I would quietly pray for grace and wisdom and bind any demons that were stirring up trouble during our communications. If you are experiencing this, you might want to look up some teachings on the spirit of leviathan. It is a demonic spirit that confuses, twists, and blocks communications. I won't elaborate here, but I recommend that you do your own research. One night, my husband and I slid into marital discord. I was doing my best to maintain an atmosphere of calm, but I was experiencing what felt like a series of pokes and prods in the form of criticisms and accusations. I tried to remain reasonable and at peace, but after about half an hour, my irritation was rising. Finally I said, "I do not think this is the time to talk about these things. I'm going to have a bath," and stormed upstairs.

Forty-five minutes later and after a long soak, I came back expecting the black cloud to have passed, but it had not. Bob picked up exactly where we had left off. I tried again to stop our trajectory down this negative, no-win path that we were traveling, but it was to no avail. I lost my temper. I could feel the Holy Spirit trying to restrain me, but I got very fleshy, and I ignored His warning. I shouted at Bob, saying, "What is the matter with you?" I stomped out of the room, up the stairs, and slammed the bedroom door with all my might. It felt so good to do that. I reasoned that this was all out of character, but then I started to feel badly. I knew and could feel that I had grieved the Holy Spirit, and I repented as best I could.

Our house was pretty quiet the next couple of days, and I suspected that it was because we had been invited to a party with some of his friends. Bob wanted us to go without the cloud of our argument hanging over us. *Fair enough*, I thought. However, it was obvious to me that some of those friends had serious misgivings about my Christian walk. I was very aware of their disdain as we left the party.

It had unexpectedly and lightly snowed, and I was wearing high-heeled party shoes. I tiptoed along the curb, which had no snow, to get to my side of the car.

Unfortunately, I had to walk up a bit of a hill to get around the door and inside the car. I slipped and fell. My arm was stuck underneath me as I fell. I knew I had done something very serious to myself. I crawled on my hands and knees, got into the car, and sat in the passenger seat, sweating profusely and feeling queasy and faint. I realized how foolish I had been. In our ongoing discord, I had not looked after my own safety. I could have asked Bob to bring the car to me on a clear driveway. In my stubbornness, I did not want to ask anything of him, and that was my sin. Fortunately, the night air was cold. I rolled down the window so that I would not pass out as we drove home. As we pulled into our driveway, I said, "We need to go to the hospital. I have done something pretty serious."

Fortunately, the entire appointment at the hospital took only forty-five minutes. I was x-rayed, which showed that I had many breaks in my left wrist. I was sent home with a temporary cast and told to come back on the following Monday—when the orthopedic surgeon would be in the clinic. At that time, they would discuss surgery with me. So I went home, praying of course.

I returned as requested. I was interviewed by the teaching head surgeon as well as some of the residents. They were ready to set up a surgery, which would involve inserting a variety of pins and bolts permanently in my wrist.

I asked, "Isn't there another way?"

They looked surprised, and one of them said, "Yes, we can do a relocation of the bones by pulling and pressure, but most people choose not to do that because it is very painful."

I asked the doctor to leave me for five minutes while I prayed. I said to my husband, "Please, put your hand on me and pray that I would hear the Lord and have His wisdom about what to do." He prayed, and I felt the Lord was saying, *I can look after this for you without surgery.* When they came back and I told them that I wanted the nonsurgical bone relocation. They were surprised and not particularly pleased. I was about to find out why.

An orderly and the young resident orthopedic surgeon were to be the ministers of my procedure. I asked the orderly several questions while he was prepping and the only one present. He did not acknowledge or answer any of my queries. I could see that he had hearing aids, and I determined that deafness was probably the problem. When he was finished, Bob came in and he too asked the orderly a question. Again there was no answer. I said to Bob, "I don't think he hears well."

The resident doctor then came in to explain what she and the orderly were going to do. I asked her if I could first pray for their skill, their wisdom, the successful placement of my bone, and my healing. She responded sweetly by saying, "My grandmother would love that." I launched into a prayer for the space that we were occupying in the hospital, the procedure, the medical staff, and me. She again left me with the orderly, who continued to get things ready.

As he was preparing, he paused at one point and looked at me. I said, trying again, "Where are you from?" This time he answered. I wondered, *Is he lip reading?*

He said, "I used to live in Afghanistan, but I have been here for decades now."

"Really? And do you have family here?"

"Yes, and children who are now adults."

"Did any of your other family members come?"

He looked sad and said, "No, and they won't come now.

They have children and grandchildren themselves. But I myself am very glad to be here."

"Did you work in a hospital there?"

"Yes," he said. Looking a little sheepish, he said, "I used to be an orthopedic surgeon there. My English was not good enough to pass the exams here in Canada, but I use my skills in this department."

At that very moment as my joy and enthusiasm bubbled over, the resident walked back in. I said, "Praise the Lord! I have not one but two orthopedic surgeons working on me together. This is awesome."

The resident looked at me in shock, then at her helper, and said, "Are you?" That started their conversation about his previously unknown medical training and history. They spoke over me, which I knew was providing relief from some of their tension.

They got to business as a team. The orderly pulled my elbow, and the young woman resident pulled my wrist and fingers. They twisted and pulled over what seemed like an agonizing eternity, until they felt that the bones were back in place. They had previously given me a muscle relaxer and an injection for pain, but the resident had assured me that it would not help very much. She was right. I had a whole new respect and empathy for the victims of torture. The pain was excruciating. It probably lasted no more than ten minutes, but it seemed to go on much longer. They worked hard at what I realized was a very physically demanding procedure. I began to understand the reason that surgeons preferred surgery and that patients might yield to surgery instead of manual adjustments.

When they were finished, my new friend from Afghanistan began to put on a cast. He was very careful and kind. He advised me, "I am going to put this cast on a little tighter than I might normally do, in an attempt to hold the bones in place. If it's loose, it's too easy for them to slide around and move out of place. You must keep your arm at about a ninety-degree angle for six weeks, because if it swells, we'll have to cut the cast off and start again. And just so you know, we can do this same procedure as many times as it takes, but it will require us to re-break the bones first. Obviously, it would be better if your bones set properly this time." He then added, "In a lot of places, people have to do it this way—the way you did." I could see a glimmer of admiration in his eyes for my courage.

As we left the room, I smiled and said to him, "I am going to be praying for you and your family, those here and at home."

He looked at me, smiled, and said, "And I will pray for you."

Each follow-up visit, we would smile at each other as I was ushered in to see a new resident, who would go over all my charts again. All of them wanted to know the reason that I had chosen the path that I did. It became a testimony that intrigued them all. The bones were healing nicely, and I gave God all the glory.

One of the many residents who took their turns to see me was a woman from Europe. She and her husband were training in different medical departments within our Canadian hospital. She began to ask me questions about my faith and the church that I went to.

I talked about Airport Church, and she said, "Oh, yes, we went there once but did not like it very much. It was a bit extreme."

I smiled and said, "The power of the Holy Spirit will

always attract people who need God in an extreme way. I assure you that it is a good church. One of the church's satellites you might try is the young adults' church down on Bloor Street. I myself have not been there, but I hear it is an exciting outreach." That was the end of our appointment.

A few months later, Conor asked me if I would come with him, as his pastor and try out the young adults' church on Bloor Street. We arrived early for the four o'clock Sunday afternoon service. You can imagine my surprise when among the handful of young people who were already there, there was the resident surgeon who had asked me so many questions about my faith and church.

I approached her, smiled, and asked, "Do you remember me? I had a broken wrist, and we talked several months ago."

She did remember. She laughed and said, "Well you told me to try this out, and here I am. My husband and I have made this our church. We just went on an encounter weekend with this group to get more personal ministry and training. It has all been wonderful. Thank you." We hugged.

As an aside, a few months after that, I heard it reported that somebody in the young adults' church had tithed over $30,000, and they were astounded. I don't know for sure, but I suspect that it was the medical couple who had come briefly from Europe. They had traveled to learn more medically, but our Lord, who does more than we can dream of or imagine, enabled them to mature spiritually as well.

While I was at home with my arm propped up, I was able to do very little. I began to use the computer and the Internet. Technology is not one of my strengths, but how much can one person read and pray? I had time. I stumbled on an online promotion for a John Maxwell leadership program called the Ninety-Day Road Map to Success. I followed the prompts and read about many facets of the course. It was a ninety-day educational program online with videos and teaching. I thought, *Why not? I have a lot of time right now.* So I paid my tuition and began the program.

It was very involved and a lot of work—much more than I had thought or expected it would be. Each participant chose a track of skill development. I have not done the entire program, but once you are involved, you can go back over the material and stay connected. I learned that John Maxwell had been a pastor for over twenty-five years before he and his team developed these leadership programs. He has authored many books on the topic of leadership, and he is a much-sought-after speaker on leadership globally.

To my astonishment and great delight, I found out much later as I was studying the course, it included a free hotel stay for their John Maxwell three-day event in Orlando, Florida. I had missed reading about that incentive in my earlier search of the package, but I was intrigued. My husband declined the spousal offer that it included, but I was determined to fly to Orlando with my newly healed wrist for the event.

It was a highly organized, wonderful conference, which hosted 2,500 people in a room that was filled with high-energy music, lights, inspirational teaching, and communal meals. All registrants had been required to prepare a five-minute talk about themselves that they would present to the other people at their assigned table. It had to be exactly five minutes, and we would be timed. We were all terrified. It was very difficult to give a speech in an exact time frame. If you went over, you were cut off. If you went under the allotted time, people looked at you until the five minutes were up. It was a very humbling assignment.

Aside from that stress, learning about other people's journeys was really interesting. We got to know each other very well and in a unique way. My talk centered on my transformation that occurred because of Jack's birth and my spirit-led faith journey. Of course by then, they all knew that I was a pastor.

Early on the second morning, all attendees were invited to participate in a church session, which was led by John Maxwell. Everyone was invited without pressure or judgement, but it was clear that it was going to be John Maxwell's pastoral presentation of his faith in Jesus Christ. Of course, I went. I was blown away. His preaching was anointed, and he ended with an altar call. When they were invited by John to "Come forward to receive Christ," two-thirds of those who were attending the service streamed down, and the helpers began distributing freely gifted Bibles. John Maxwell began to cry a little. The atmosphere was charged. I felt much like I had at one of Benny Hinn's huge Toronto, Canada, meetings, except that John was reaching powerfully into the business community. What a gift he had.

On the last day of my stay, I went outside to reflect on my experience and the event. I sat beside the hotel pool, which was ringed magnificently with exotic garden landscaping and several waterfalls. We had each been given a gift as a takeaway, which was a bound, black hardcover book inscribed with gold letters that said, *The Greatest Story Ever Told*. The pages inside were blank.

During the event, John Maxwell had related his own story of being given such a book and encouraged to write in it by his secretary. It was an important start of his prolific writing career. Anyone can find his many books in bookstores' business sections or online. He instructed us all to *tell our stories* and write them out, even if it was only for us.

Truly, I now agree that everyone's life is an interesting tale and that the journey is more interesting and important than the destination. Hopefully, we will grow and change for the better, forcing everyone and everything around us to change. God is the Author and Finisher of our faith. He is constantly at work, raising his spiritual family of children and changing us to the image of His Son. The seed for the book that you are reading was planted at this conference.

The possibility of marketplace ministry was now a potent image, which percolated in my mind. I often asked the Lord to direct the things that I should be doing with my time. While attending a family wedding, I met a talented floral artist who encouraged me to join the Toronto Flower and Garden Club. In their mandatory flower-arranging classes, I sat with another woman in the back row. We spent a lot of time laughing at our feeble artistic endeavors. This woman ultimately became an answer to my need for a naturally based skin-care line. I had only been using gentle oatmeal soap and water because of my skin affliction in 2011. My dermatologist had warned me about the many toxic chemicals that were in most creams and cosmetics and gave firm instructions not to use them.

My floral-class friend then introduced me to Arbonne health and beauty products. I purchased the botanical skin-care line, and a month later, I took used it on an intercessor's trip around Israel with the End-Time Handmaidens and Servants. The trip was spiritually fulfilling, and I came home impressed and happy with the results of my new skin-care regime.

Four months later, my floral-class friend delivered Arbonne products that I had ordered in a special promotion. She looked at me very doubtfully as we talked and posed a simple question. "You wouldn't want to sell this, would you?"

I was about to give my somewhat prideful, immediate response of, "No!" I wanted to do God's work. To my surprise, the Holy Spirit firmly and clearly said, *You do.* I was shocked, and it obviously showed on my face. My friend saw my conflicted, emotional reaction and asked what was going on. She is a Roman Catholic, so I felt reasonably safe to share what I had just heard. I told her my spiritual revelation. In obedience to the Holy Spirit's directive, I would join the business.

She laughed heartily and said, "I have heard many reasons why people want to sell this business and these product lines, but I have never heard that one."

As I began my new enterprise as an Arbonne independent consultant, I admit that I did not work terribly hard at it. I enjoyed doing spiritual Christian things much more, but slowly, my personal business began to take shape. I learned more about the products and then tried their thirty-day nutritional program. I was astounded with the results. Years of aches and pains that I had attributed to damage from carrying Jack disappeared after two weeks. As a nice little side bonus, I lost seven pounds. I realized that the low-glycemic index of their food plan and products worked together to detoxify and remove a lot of my inflammation. I was sleeping better, having more energy, and set free from my black-tea caffeine addiction. I was a product convert.

My husband watched me during my November 2017 Arbonne cleanse and suggested that we do the detox thirty-day program together after the New Year. He lost thirteen pounds, but more importantly, he was able to stop taking his blood-pressure medications.

I realized that in the wisdom of God, He had given me a key to help others restore and maintain physical health. Many beautiful and spiritual Christians have a diet and lifestyle that need adjusting, if they are to continue serving the Lord in ministry many more years. The Bible says, "We go from strength to strength,"(Psalm 84:7a) but that infers that we have a body that can carry that strength. Today, most of my Arbonne business is targeted at restoring Christians to health by addressing eating habits, as I continue in spiritual discipleship, prayer, and missions. We are body, soul, and spirit, and the Lord desires that each part of us receives His healing touch.

In 2019, I went to my first Arbonne convention in Las Vegas. I had never been to that city, although now, I know that I need to pray for it. The MGM stadium was full of over eighteen thousand healthy, excited consultants from six different countries. All I could see was a youthful, talented, and potential harvest field, and I thought, *What a clever, gracious, and wise God we serve.* He is reaching out everywhere that He can with the offer of forgiveness, restored purpose, and life.

In the book of Acts, the exploits of Jesus Christ's disciples are relayed to us. I believe every Holy Spirit-filled believer and disciple can follow and do great exploits in

His name. A great exchange is available to anyone and everyone who calls on the name of Jesus Christ. We can all see that mankind is capable of great wickedness. Some people cause much suffering on the earth, and it hurts the heart of our Father. In His love, He sent his Son as the human incarnation of the Godhead to be our Savior. Jesus willingly carried upon Himself the sins of all people of all times and then paid the price with His life to set us free. It was a very high price. He is love, and His love declares that you are worth all that He suffered. He came to rescue, heal, and set us free. This is His great desire, delight, and a manifestation of His limitless wisdom, goodness, and power.

Jesus Christ, the perfect Lamb of God, shed His blood and died for you and me. Long ago, He and His Father planned and provided for our rescue and rehabilitation. Jesus gave us all that He is. By faith as we receive His gift of love and forgiveness and accept His sacrifice on the cross for us, and our old nature dies with Him. We can then begin afresh as a born-again child of God, who is willing to learn and surrender to new ways—His ways.

Before going to the cross, Jesus prayed and asked His Father to protect us, fill us with joy and sanctify us through His Word (see John 17). Truth is Christ given and Holy Spirit imparted. His word is truth.

Today's world is in turmoil, as has happened so many times before in history. The prophet Isaiah's words still holds true, where he says that wicked people take counsel together against the Lord but that it will ultimately come to nothing. This idea is repeated in Psalm 2. Their evil plans will not stand, for God sees everything, and He is undertaking to bring correction, order, and His kingdom to reign through His anointed believers. We assist in this struggle of His light overcoming darkness.

Many times in His Word, the Lord repeats that we should not be afraid of the wicked. The Lord of Hosts is the one that we lift up, and He is our hope, sanctuary, and safe place (see Isaiah 8:8–14). The abiding presence of our almighty God goes with the family of people who choose Him. Love and seek Him, be blessed, and be a blessing to the earth.

Recently, I had a wonderful vision that I believe is a prophetic invitation to all of us. I was looking into a gray, foggy atmosphere, when I noticed a glimmer of light in the midst of it. As I focused on it, I could see an illuminated figure of a man with a shawl-covered head and long robe approaching. I realized that as the figure became brighter and closer, it was Jesus. His hand was extended palm upward in an invitation. Would I accept His hand?

His eyes seemed to search through me in His intense but loving gaze, as He said, *Come.* I could feel an impartation of courage and strength. Beloved, you and I have a choice. Will we step out of our known but self-absorbed comfort zone into the supernatural realm of our God and Father? This zone has healing and miracles. Here His kingdom comes to and through us.

Let us encourage one another. Jesus will not let go of us, and He declares that He is always victorious. He will touch our broken places, bring healing and wholeness, and invite us to co-labor with Him to bring heaven to earth.

We can walk on the real substance of His Word. His love, grace, and power are available to us. Let us respond, by telling him, *Lord, I am going with You. I will walk in Your Word, will, and way. Let the adventure begin!*

ABOUT THE AUTHOR

This mother of three beautiful children faced a crisis when her fourth son, Jack was born profoundly disabled. Moving through every emotion from disbelief to doubt, **Laurel Hobbs** started down a road of spiritual discovery that forever changed the way she looks at her Christian faith, her relationship with God and her personal relationships with others. Her experiences and remarkable insights are changing the way Christians view their own challenges and offers hope in difficult situations.

Laurel Hobbs earned a Fine Arts degree and an MBA from York University, Toronto, Canada. After setting up and managing a one year showcase of the arts for York, she then enjoyed six successful years in advertising. She has been married for 40 years and is an ordained pastor, a home-church host, a women's ministry leader, serves on education and ministry boards and has enjoyed short term missions to many countries around the globe. She and her husband, Bob, have three other married sons and seven grandchildren.

CPSIA information can be obtained
at www.ICGtesting.com
Printed in the USA
FSHW010324181121
86259FS